ARISTOPHANES AND ATHENIAN SOCIETY
OF THE EARLY
FOURTH CENTURY B.C.

MNEMOSYNE

BIBLIOTHECA CLASSICA BATAVA

COLLEGERUNT

A. D. LEEMAN · H. W. PLEKET · C. J. RUIJGH

BIBLIOTHECAE FASCICULOS EDENDOS CURAVIT

C. J. RUIJGH, KLASSIEK SEMINARIUM, OUDE TURFMARKT 129, AMSTERDAM

SUPPLEMENTUM OCTOGESIMUM PRIMUM

E. DAVID

ARISTOPHANES AND ATHENIAN SOCIETY OF THE EARLY FOURTH CENTURY B.C.

LUGDUNI BATAVORUM   E. J. BRILL   MCMLXXXIV

ARISTOPHANES AND ATHENIAN SOCIETY OF THE EARLY FOURTH CENTURY B.C.

BY

E. DAVID

LEIDEN   E.   J.   BRILL 1984

Publication of this volume was made possible by a grant from the Haifa University Press

ISBN   90 04 07062 1

PRINTED IN THE NETHERLANDS BY E. J. BRILL

*To the memory of
my grandmother,
Henriette Landau*

CONTENTS

Foreword IX

Introduction 1
1. Historical Background...................................... 3
2. Poverty: Symptoms, Ideas regarding Solutions and Criticism
   of Ideas 5
3. Poverty versus Riches...................................... 14
4. The Sources of the "Communistic" Ideas 20
5. *Misthos Ekklesiastikos* 29
6. The Censure of Materialism.. 32
7. The Middle Road.. 38

Bibliography 44

FOREWORD

In this short monograph, I have tried to address myself to the classicist as well as the general reader. Philological discussions and Greek quotations have normally been restricted to the footnotes. When used in the text, Greek terms have been translitterated and explained.

The abbreviations for ancient authors and collections of source material are the conventional ones, as used, for example, in the *Oxford Classical Dictionary*. Titles of journals are usually abbreviated as in *L'Année Philologique*.

My thanks are due to the University of Haïfa for its generous assistance in the publication.

Introduction

The last two extant plays of Aristophanes—the *Ekklesiazousai* and the *Ploutos*—have often raised questions as to their author's intellectual and artistic abilities. Many scholars have spoken of these two plays in terms of a decline in Aristophanes' art and have connected the decline with personal fatigue or with the political situation of Athens after her defeat in the Peloponnesian War. Moreover, the *Ekklesiazousai* and the *Ploutos* have often been underestimated or neglected as historical sources. It has been argued, among other things, that the plays contain neither a social lesson nor a serious criticism of ideas, but are to be taken at their best as mere fantasies.[1]

Despite the authority of their supporters—many of them eminent scholars—these views do not seem to be well founded. The Aristophanes of the last plays is certainly different from the Aristophanes of earlier comedies, but difference need not signify decline. After her defeat in the

---

[1] See, e.g., M. Croiset, *Aristophanes and the Political Parties at Athens* (London, 1909), p. 177: "It (i.e., *Eccl.*) seeks neither to construct theories nor to overthrow them"; p. 181f.: "This short summary shows clearly how far the play (i.e., *Plut.*) is from being a serious argument and from containing or declaring a social doctrine ... All this proves that the social lesson of the *Plutus* amounts to very little"; G. Norwood, *Greek Comedy* (London, 1931), p. 265f.; 275; G. Murray, *Aristophanes* (Oxford, 1933), p. 198: "It would be quite a mistake to regard the play (i.e., *Eccl.*) as a serious criticism of ideas of which Aristophanes disapproved"; cf. p. 198, where it is said to belong to the "literature of fatigue" and p. 207, where *Plut.* is considered no more than "a fairly amusing play"; cf. H. Van Daele, *Aristophane* V (Paris, Budé, 1963), p. 11: "Fiction ingénieuse, fantaisie amusante ... l'*Assemblée des Femmes* n'a point d'autre portée"; p. 78: "*Ploutos* ... est une pure fantaisie ... L'auteur n'y expose aucune thèse ...". For a more extreme approach, see A. E. Taylor, *Plato* (London, 1926), p. 210: "... the broken man ... who could sink to the tiresome dirtiness of the *Ecclesiazusae*"; L. Strauss, *Socrates and Aristophanes* (New-York, 1966), p. 279: "It is not sufficient to say that the *Assembly of Women* is the ugliest comedy; it is *the* ugly comedy"; But later, p. 295, Strauss states that "... the *Ploutos* is in its way as ugly as the *Assembly of Women*." To be sure, there are a few exceptions to these attitudes towards Aristophanes' last plays. One of the most significant exceptions is R. G. Ussher's commentary—*Aristophanes, Ecclesiazusae* (Oxford, 1973). Ussher praises the literary quality of the play, yet argues that it "is not intended to inculcate any kind of message" (p. XXXIV and n. 2; cf. p. XXX and n. 2). See also *id. Aristophanes*, Greece & Rome, New Surveys in the Classics, 13 (Oxford, 1979), p. 14; 18f. The importance of Aristophanes' last extant plays as major historical sources has been pointed out by several scholars; see esp. F. Sartori, "Elementi storici del tardo teatro aristofanico e documentazione contemporanea", in Akten des VI. Internationalen Kongresses für griechische und lateinische Epigraphik, *Vestigia* 17 (München, 1973), p. 328ff. However, this paper deals with the socio-economic problems only in a very general manner. As far as I know, there is no comprehensive study devoted to the analysis of these problems in Aristophanes' last extant plays.

Peloponnesian War, Athens had also undergone complex processes of change, but whatever one may think of her decline as a great power, or of her acute socio-economic problems, the culture that the Athenians produced in the fourth century B.C., though in many respects different from that of their fifth-century predecessors, can hardly be considered as inferior.

It is not our main purpose here to attempt a rehabilitation of the "purely" literary value of Aristophanes' last plays, although I believe they have too often been underestimated and misjudged as works of art. Our central aim is to set forth their value as historical sources and to show that they do contain a significant social message. In the following pages we propose to identify and analyze the problems of Athenian society with which the plays are concerned and to examine Aristophanes' views on the essence of these problems as well as on the attempts to find satisfactory solutions. However, we hope that the discussion of these issues will also throw some light on the intrinsic value of the plays as works of art, assuming that a central purpose of art in general, and dramatic art in particular, is—and I believe it is—as Shakespeare defined it: to be the mirror of an age, "to show virtue her own feature, scorn her own image, and the very age and body of the time his form and pressure."

---

[2] The dating of the *Eccl.* rests mainly on l. 193, where an alliance (τὸ συμμαχικόν) is mentioned, and on the scholiast quoting (*ad loc.*) Philochoros' statement that an alliance was formed between the Spartans and Boiotians two years before the production of the play. (Since such an alliance is impossible, "Spartans" is commonly taken to be a textual error and emended as "Athenians"). See Philoch. *FGrHist* 328 F148. If this alliance is taken as the anti-Spartan league formed in 395/4 B.C., then 392 B.C. is the year of the production. But if the alliance is understood as that formed by Athens and Thebes in 396/5 B.C. (i.e., before the battle of Haliartos), then the production has to be dated a year earlier (393 B.C.). The first view is shared by most scholars. See, e.g., J. van Leeuwen, *Aristophanis Ecclesiazusae* (Leyden, 1905), *Prolegomena*, p. XVIII; Croiset, *op. cit.* p. 165, n. 2; Wilamowitz, *Aristophanes Lysistrate, Beilage: Ekklesiazusen* (Berlin, 1927), p. 203; H. Van Daele, *op. cit.* p. 5, n. 1; more recently, Sartori, *op. cit.* p. 330. For the second view, see B. B. Rogers, *The Ecclesiazusae of Aristophanes* (London, 1902), p. XX; Ussher, *Eccl. Commentary*, p. XXIff., with detailed discussion and further literature; cf. however the review of Ussher by D. M. MacDowell, *JHS* 94 (1974), p. 184f., who admits that this view may be correct, but argues that its presentation by Ussher is "too dogmatic". There are many historical allusions in the play (see Ussher, *ibid.*); they do not help to indicate a precise date but point to the late 390s; cf. K. J. Dover, *Aristophanic Comedy* (Berkeley and Los Angeles, 1972), p. 190. The date of the *Ploutos'* production is commonly accepted as 388 B.C. See, e.g., B. B. Rogers, *The Plutus of Aristophanes* (London, 1907), p. VIIff.; Croiset, *op. cit.* p. 177 and n. 1, with detailed discussion; Van Daele, *op cit.* p. 75; Murray, *Aristophanes*, p. 199; Dover, *ibid.* p. 202; Th. Gelzer, *RE* Suppl. XII (1970), s.v. "Aristophanes" col. 1505.

1. Historical Background

The age mirrored in Aristophanes' last plays is, as already stated, that of the generation following Athens' defeat by Sparta in the Peloponnesian War. About a decade after the defeat, Athens became involved in a new war against Sparta—the Corinthian War, and this time two of Sparta's former allies in Greece, Thebes and Corinth—Athens' bitterest enemies in the recent past—were now fighting on her side against the Spartans. Both plays—the *Ekklesiazousai* and the *Ploutos*—were composed during this war: the first in 393 or 392 B.C., the second in 388 B.C.[2]

Where internal matters were concerned, Athens and other Greek cities were faced, during the opening decades of the fourth century, with severe social problems. An acute economic crisis was felt in many Greek cities which had participated in the Peloponnesian War. Recovery from the cruel blows of this war was extremely difficult, especially in view of the fact that within less than a decade they were again engaged in a large-scale war.[3]

The agrarian sector of the economy had the most ruinous damage inflicted on it, although other sectors too, especially mining, were, for a time, seriously affected. However, those who suffered most, economically, were the farmers, owners of small or moderate estates, who constituted a kind of an agrarian middle class. These social elements, which had previously formed one of the cornerstones of economic stability in Attika and elsewhere, were now faced with difficulties with which, in many cases, they could not cope. Many of them lost all hope of improving the situation in their fields. Some were compelled to sell their estates; others could not even do that, since their land was in such poor condition as a result of the devastation caused by the war: as a result they decided to abandon it. Those who had tried, in spite of everything, to rehabilitate themselves by means of loans were often hopelessly burdened with debt and, sooner or later, became paupers. After having abandoned, sold or lost their land, these agrarian elements were to join the ranks of the agricultural or urban proletariat. Some of them were compelled to work for low salaries, others were unemployed, since the cheaper labour force of the slaves was often preferred to that of freemen.

---

[3] See K. J. Beloch, *Griechische Geschichte* [2]III, I (Berlin-Leipzig, 1922), p. 263ff.; 313ff.; 427ff.; G. Busolt, *Griechische Staatskunde* I (München, 1920), p. 169ff.; G. Glotz, *Le travail dans la Grèce ancienne* (Paris, 1920), p. 175ff.; W. E. Heitland, *Agricola* (Cambridge, 1921), p. 28ff.; C. Mossé, *Athens in Decline* (London, 1973), p. 12ff.; A. Fuks, "Patterns and Types of Social-Economic Revolution in Greece from the Fourth to the Second Century B.C.", *Anc. Soc.* 5 (1974), p. 54ff., with further literature. For the social problems of Sparta during the first decades following the Peloponnesian War, see E. David, *Sparta between Empire and Revolution* (New York, Arno Press, 1981), p. 50ff.

A small group of citizens succeeded in exploiting the economic crisis and increased their wealth by lending money, by investing capital, or by speculating over neglected lands, as well as by various other means. A considerable amount of wealth was accumulated by a few in trade, business and monetary transactions. With the decline of the small and moderate type of property—a process paralleled by the formation of large estates, or the growth of a quasi-capitalistic type of Greek industry—the middle class gradually decreased.

The growing polarity between excessive wealth and abject poverty began to destroy the socio-economic equilibrium that had been prevalent in most Greek cities since the end of the archaic period. The prosperity of a small section within the citizen-body and the luxurious life-style of the wealthy threw into even greater relief the economic distress and pauperization of large sections of citizens in Athens and in other Greek cities. Consequently, there was an increasing hostility on the part of the masses towards the rich, especially towards the *nouveaux riches*. All these factors engendered an acute and complex social conflict, which was to precipitate the decline of the city-state.

Aristophanes' last extant plays provide precious evidence for the historical analysis of contemporary socio-economic problems and of ideas regarding various possible solutions. The plays reveal also the author's reaction to the social reality as well as to the contemporary mentality and patterns of thought.

In the *Ekklesiazousai* a gynaecocracy is founded on the premise that all other devices have already been tried without success and that women are the most conservative section of society. Paradoxically, the new regime brings about the most radical change in the socio-economic order through the abolition of private property and of the family.

Thus Aristophanes has again taken the theme of women's initiative in public life—a theme already treated in earlier plays (*Lysistrata* and *Thesmophoriazousai*)—and this time has combined it with the idea of collectivism.

Under the newly proposed feminist "communism", all citizens, women and men alike, are to enjoy an equal share in property and in the sexual pleasures (and displeasures) of life. All goods, movable and immovable alike, are to be held in common: land, money and whatever other property the citizens happen to possess. Absolute civic community (*koinōnia*)—meaning common property, common use and common sexual life—is enforced. This "communist" system applies to consumption, not to production: work is left only for the slaves.[4]

---

[4] See P. Vidal-Naquet, "Esclavage et gynécocratie dans la tradition, le mythe et l'utopie", *Recherches sur les structures sociales dans l'antiquité classique* (Paris, 1970), p. 79. The

Four years after having presented and refuted the idea of salvation through this kind of "communism", the playwright gave his audience the illusion of salvation through the healing of the blind god of wealth – Ploutos. His eyesight is restored and all social ills disappear, since Wealth now gives a share only to those who deserve it.

Despite the difference in the subject matter, the historical background and the socio-economic topics of both plays are basically similar.[5] Therefore a considerable part of the discussion will have to deal with both plays together, as if they were a single work.

2. *Poverty: Symptoms, Ideas regarding Solutions and Criticism of Ideas*

It has been suggested that Aristophanes was indifferent to the subject of the poverty of the masses and its consequences.[6] However, the problem of poverty is essential to the social background of the *Ekklesiazousai* and of the *Ploutos*. It is essential even from the dramatic point of view, since in both plays the plot is based on various ideas of salvation from the condition of poverty.[7] The symptoms of poverty are summed up by Chremylos, the elderly farmer who is the leading character of the *Ploutos*, in a pithy description of "blessings": "What do you ever offer? Blisters from the public-bath stove? A crowd of scrawny, old women and starving children? Countless lice, mosquitos and fleas that buzz around the head all night and worry one, waking him up and telling him: 'You will starve, but get up!' And, in addition to these, you give rags to wear instead of clothes, instead of a bed a rush mattress with bugs that awaken even the soundest of sleepers; instead of a carpet a rotten mat; instead of a pillow a big stone; and to feed: mallow shoots instead of bread and instead of barley, radish leaves; instead of a chair the head of a broken jar; instead

---

author stresses the significance of placing the slaves outside the community, even by revolutionary or utopic schemes. He mentions Aristotle's basic differentiation between women and slaves (*Pol.* 1252 b1ff.) and remarks: "L'utopie aristophanesque peut en faire la moitié supérieure de la cité, de même que Platon pourra les placer presque sur le même plan que les hommes, mais les esclaves, eux, ne sont pas de la cité du tout et tout se passe comme si la mythologie, la tradition légendaire aussi bien que l'utopie tenaient compte de ce fait"; cf. M. I. Finley, "Utopianism, Ancient and Modern", *The Use and Abuse of History* (London, 1975), p. 187.

[5] This has been rightly stressed by Rogers, *Plutus*, p. XIIIf. The similarity was wrongly interpreted by D. Greene, "The Comic Technique of Aristophanes", *Hermathena* 50 (1937), p. 124, who strangely regarded communism as the "entire theme" of the *Ploutos*.

[6] See, for instance, A. Couat, *Aristophane et l'ancienne comédie attique* (Paris, 1902), p. 195: "Il n'a pour eux (i.e., les pauvres) ni pitié ni sympathie profonde et attristée, car leur condition lui paraît supportable ... Il ne voit du reste dans cette misère que la souffrance physique; il n'a pas l'air d'en sentir la laideur morale ..." (However, see below, p. 35ff.) cf. Th. Gelzer, "Aristophanes" (above, n. 2), col. 1500: "Die Identifikation des Dichters mit dem δῆμος und mit der σωτηρία τῆς πόλεως ... fehlt den Ekklesiazusen"; cf. coll. 1502f.

[7] On salvation, see below, esp. nn. 99-105.

of a kneading-trough the broken rib of a cask. Now tell me, have I shown you as the cause of many blessings to all men?''[8]

Yes, one may answer, he has provided the audience with a summary of the eternal, well-known symptoms of abject poverty: hunger, dearth of clothes, dearth of proper housing, deplorable sanitary conditions—all the ''blessings'' of a miserable life. These symptoms of poverty are mentioned time and again both in the *Ekklesiazousai* and in the *Ploutos*. The most distressing among them is hunger. Allusions to the gravity of this problem are to be found in contemporary literature. In his speech *On the Peace with Sparta*—composed shortly after the *Ekklesiazousai* (391 B.C.)—Andokides expresses the state of mind prevalent in Athens when he mentions one of the arguments which has been raised in the discussion concerning the peace proposals, namely that walls, even if recovered, cannot feed the Athenians.[9]

In Aristophanes' last plays it is possible to see that for many Athenians at that time, salvation meant, first and foremost, finding a solution to the problem of food supplies.

This is certainly true in the case of Blepyros, the husband of the leading character in the *Ekklesiazousai*, Praxagora. Before hearing his wife's revolutionary programme, he envisages a proposal in much more limited and modest terms, as befits his level of intelligence. According to this proposal, all corn merchants will freely give each pauper an adequate quantity of barley for a good dinner.[10]

Aristophanes has taken the food motif, a comic motif traditionally connected with the theme of a golden age,[11] and has given it new dimensions in his last plays.

When presenting her programme, Praxagora takes care to emphasize that in the new regime no one will be motivated by need, the need of food in particular.[12] She is aware that stopping the food allowance and making one's stomach suffer is the most convincing punishment.[13] On the other

---

[8] *Plut.* 535-47.

[9] Andoc. 3 (*Pax*), 36; cf. U. Albini, *Andoc. De pace* (Firenze, 1964), p. 107f. (*ad loc.*).

[10] *Eccl.* 424-5.

[11] See Athen. 6, 267E-270 A, with quotations from several comic poets dealing with this theme: Kratinos, *Ploutoi* = Th. Kock, *Comicorum Atticorum Fragmenta* I (Leipzig, 1880), fr. 165 (hereafter cited by editor's name); Krates, *Wild animals* = Kock, I, fr. 14-15; Telekleides, *Amphiktyons* = Kock, I, fr. 1; Pherekrates, *Miners* = Kock, I, fr. 108; *id. Persians* = Kock, I, fr. 130; Aristoph. *Broilers* = Kock, I, fr. 508; Metagenes, *Thurio-Persians* = Kock, I, fr. 6; Nikophon, *Sirens* = Kock, I, fr. 13. For the significance of the food motif in Attic comedy, see especially V. Ehrenberg, *The People of Aristophanes. A Sociology of Old Attic Comedy*[2] (Oxford, 1951), p. 319ff.

[12] *Eccl.* 588; 605ff.; and see below.

[13] *Eccl.* 665f.; cf. Metagenes *ap.* Athen. 6, 271A = Kock, I, fr. 9.

hand, she knows very well that abundance of food will be the most efficient way to get support for her schemes. Under the new regime, the most eminent public places in the city, those formerly used for public activities, will have a new function—places of food consumption: all the lawcourts and arcades will be converted into dining halls, the speakers' platforms will serve for the wine jars and mixing bowls, while the lot-casting urns devised for the allocation of jurors to the popular courts of justice will be set up in the Agora and will assign dinner places at the copious banquets to be held at the common messes. After elaborating on the last point, Praxagora finds it proper to reassure the audience that there will be enough food and drink for everybody.[14]

Behind the grotesque transformation of the political function into the gastronomical is not only a *reductio ad absurdum* of the solution to the hunger problem, but also the playwright's reaction to the growing mentality of egocentric materialism in contemporary Athenian society. This aspect will be dealt with later in a more detailed manner.

There is an obsession with food and with the idea of food in the *Ekklesiazousai*, and the issue is also prominent in the *Ploutos*, as it can be seen in Chremylos' words quoted above[15]—the description of Poverty's "blessings"—and in many other passages in the play. Mention is made, for instance, of men who look like wasps because of hunger.[16] When told about the existence of many honest men who had no bread to eat,[17] a great section of Aristophanes' audience could perfectly understand the idea from personal experience. And this is true not only with respect to honest men. Amongst the hideous gallery of figures presented in the *Ploutos*, there is a gigolo who is capable of asking for money from an old woman in order to buy a coat, shoes or food for himself and his family. On her part the woman tries to tempt the gigolo by sending him a cake and sweets.[18]

Even the priest of Asklepios is stealing food within his temple: at night, when he believes the patients to be sleeping, he is busy removing the cakes and dried figs from the holy table and the altars; he "consecrates" the food by putting it into his bag.[19] Karion, Chremylos' slave—who is,

---

[14] *Eccl.* 676-90. This presentation has obvious affinities with the various descriptions of the abundance of food in the "golden-age" theme, as developed in the remaining fragments of the comic poets cited above, in n. 11.

[15] See above, n. 8.

[16] *Plut.* 562.

[17] *Plut.* 218f.; cf. 503f.; 627ff.; 750ff.

[18] *Plut.* 981ff. The sums he asked for a cloak (20 drachmas) and for a pair of shoes (8 drachmas) seem to be above the usual price; see Rogers, *Plutus*, p. 111 (*ad loc.*).

[19] *Plut.* 668-81.

by the way, one of the main characters in Aristophanes' last extant play [19a]—sees him in action since hunger prevents him from sleeping.

After Wealth has regained his sight, those who do not deserve to be given a share in prosperity are said to suffer from hunger: the sycophant is "hunger mad"; the god Hermes is made to complain that nobody sacrifices to him anymore and therefore he is hungry; so are also Zeus and his priest.[20] On the other hand, the healing of the god's sight, which meant salvation for the poor, was blessed above all because it solved the problem of hunger: "Come on, now, all of you, dance, leap and celebrate. For no one will tell you when coming home that there is no barley in the bin."[21]

Chremylos' argument about the possibility of saturation in everything except for the lust for wealth is dramatically developed by means of *stichomythia*, presenting an amusing parallelism and contrast between spiritual and material elements. The material side of the picture, typically, is based only on food:

Chremylos: Of all other things one may have too much: of love
Karion: Of bread –
Chremylos: Of music –
Karion: Of sweets –
Chremylos: Of honour –
Karion: Of cakes –
Chremylos: Of valour –
Karion: Of figs –
Chremylos: Of ambition –
Karion: Of barley –
Chremylos: Of command –
Karion: Of soup –

[19a] Karion's prominent role in the *Ploutos* balances that of his master. There is no precedent of such a slave role in Aristophanes' comedies; see Gelzer, "Aristophanes" (above, n. 6), col. 1510 and esp. Dover, *Aristophanic Comedy*, p. 204ff. His self-confidence is more appropriate to a citizen than to a slave. Contemporary critics of the Athenian democracy stressed the self-confidence of slaves in Athens and argued that they were treated as if they were freemen and citizens; see, e.g., Ps.-Xen. *Ath. Pol.* 1, 10-12; Xen. *Hell.* 2, 3, 48 (Theramenes' speech); Plat. *Resp.* 563B. In the case of Karion, his self confidence may in particular reflect a typical trait of a special category of slaves—those who had assisted the democrats against the Thirty in the struggle for the restoration of democracy. The audience could identify Karion as a representative of those slaves who had fought with Thrasyboulos' troops at Phyle (see *Plut.* 1146; cf. Sartori, "Elementi storici" (above, n. 1), p. 332). Thrasyboulos' subsequent motion to give citizenship to all metics and slaves who had helped the democrats failed due to the opposition of Archinos (Arist. *Ath. Pol.* 40, 2). On Karion, see also below, esp. nn. 67; 193.

[20] *Plut.* 873; 1112ff.; 1120ff.; 1172ff.

[21] *Plut.* 762f.; cf. esp. 627ff.; 802ff. The last passage stresses the abundance motif, characteristic of the golden-age theme; see above, n. 11.

Chremylos: But no one ever has enough of you (viz., wealth) ...[22]

The hungry do not think in abstract terms; they think of food. But this physical need is satiable, and so are those needs of the soul, which are expressed in abstract notions. Only the love of wealth knows no limit. Thus, based on the experience of his own time—the egocentric materialism prevalent in contemporary Athenian society—Aristophanes draws conclusions of universal impact. He seems to have regarded abject poverty as one of the factors which impelled the universal lust for wealth to its extreme in Athenian society of the early fourth century.[23]

Dearth of clothes is another acute symptom of pauperism frequently mentioned in Aristophanes' last plays alongside the problem of hunger. Mention is made, for instance, of children running about naked,[24] of people who are poor and naked,[25] of men possessing only one cloak,[26] of tattered old coats, of clumsy boots,[27] etc.

This aspect is particularly stressed in that scene of the *Ekklesiazousai* which presents the proposal of Euaion.[28] First of all, the audience has to be impressed by his personal appearance, when, as he comes forward to speak, the holes and threadbare aspect of his cloak make him seem naked, although he maintains that he is wearing a cloak or what is left of it. For a man in his deplorable state of poverty, his own salvation may be

---

[22] *Plut.* 189-93.

[23] Cf. Y. Urbain, "Les idées économiques d'Aristophane", *AC* 8 (1939), p. 185ff., credits Aristophanes with the precocious knowledge of modern laws of economics, a theory which is hardly convincing. In this specific case, he attributes to the comic poet the discovery of the "saturation law": "Comme les manuels modernes, Aristophane enseigne que la saturation des besoins déterminés est possible. Le besoin de l'argent est insatiable, parce qu'il ne correspond pas à un besoin particulier puisque l'argent peut toujours être changé contre un bien quelconque."

[24] *Eccl.* 92: "γυμνὰ δ'ἐστί μοι τὰ παιδία".

[25] *Eccl.* 566: Praxagora stresses that under the new regime "none will be poor and naked anymore". ("μὴ γυμνὸν εἶναι, μὴ πένητα μηδένα")

[26] *Eccl.* 353 (cf. 315). In this case the lack of spare clothes is also a vital element from the dramatic point of view, logically connected with the plot. However, this is not an isolated example, but it is in line with many other references to this symptom of poverty; cf. Ussher, *Eccl.* p. 125 (*ad loc.*).

[27] *Eccl.* 850; cf. *Plut.* 540; 714; 842-49; 882; 935ff. On the dearth of clothes as a symptom of poverty, see also Isocr. *Areop.* 54. The oration is much later than Aristophanes' last plays (c. 355 B.C.), which may show that the situation had not improved in the meantime. See also below the references concerning the cloak thieves.

[28] *Eccl.* 408. On Euaion, see Rogers, *Eccl.* p. 65 (*ad loc.*); Van Daele, *Aristophane*, V, p. 33, n. 3: "... le nom n'est peut-être qu'un sobriquet par antiphrase: ce mot signifie 'heureuse existence'", but see Ussher, *Eccl.* p. 132 (*ad loc.*): "the epithet implies 'who really knows what he is about', a capable man in his profession. Euaeon is well versed in all the tricks of poverty and also a good speaker ... It is this forwardness, and not his poverty, that Ar. is mocking." However, the purpose of this episode seems to be much deeper than simply to mock Euaion, since it is closely connected, as we shall try to show, with some of the main themes in the play: the condition of poverty, the ideas of salvation and the poet's reaction to these ideas.

bought for the price of a cloak—four staters. He admits this, but argues nevertheless that he is able to advise the *polis* on the ways of her salvation.[29] His solution reflects a projection of his own needs on to the whole state, which is understandable if many Athenian citizens were in a situation similar to his own. The passage containing his proposals can, therefore, show us the miserable conditions of a large section of contemporary Athenian society: "At the beginning of the winter the clothiers should give warm cloaks to everyone in need, so that no one would get pleurisy. And those who have not got beds or blankets should be allowed to sleep at the furriers' shops, after having washed themselves. Anyone who shuts his door on them in wintry weather should be fined three blankets."[30]

Euaion's motion anticipates the more radical and general programme of Praxagora. When told about Euaion's proposals, Blepyros adds his own amendment, which, as we have seen, was formulated in the same spirit, though it dealt with food supplies.[31] Praxagora herself takes care to mention clothes alongside food as basic goods which, under the new regime, no citizen will be denied the privilege of having.[32]

Euaion's words remind the audience of an additional symptom of poverty—disease. Those suffering from pleurisy and other diseases due to the deplorable conditions in which they were living could hardly find a doctor to take care of them. When Chremylos is told by Blepsidemos, his friend—in the *Ploutos*—that they have to call a doctor to take care of Wealth's sight, the answer is that there are no doctors in the city since there is no pay to offer them.[33] Even allowing—here as elsewhere—for some exaggeration due to the very nature of Aristophanes' *genre*, the essential significance of such a statement should not be underestimated. Doctors practised as state employees only in those places where the salaries were satisfactory, and it appears that during the period under discussion, Athens could not afford to pay public doctors adequate salaries.

The high frequency of certain diseases and the lack of adequate medical treatment could only bring about a considerable increase in the mortality rate, and this problem was particularly grave in view of the great losses in human lives that Athens had already suffered during the

---

[29] *Eccl.* 408-14. The price of the cloak—4 staters (= 16 drachmae: see Arist. fr. 529, Rose) is lower than the price mentioned in *Plut.* 982. See above, n. 18.

[30] *Eccl.* 415-21.

[31] See above, n. 10.

[32] *Eccl.* 566; 606f.; 653f.

[33] *Plut.* 406-408; cf. *Eccl.* 364-68; see J. P. Mahaffy, *Social Life in Greece from Homer to Menander* (London, 1898), p. 292ff.; Rogers, *Plut.* p. 46 (*ad loc.*); K. Holzinger, *Kommentar zu Aristophanes' Plutos* (Wien and Leipzig, 1940), p. 156f. (*ad loc.*).

Peloponnesian War: at the time of the *Ekklesiazousai* Athens was left with only 30,000 citizens,[33a] which means that during less than forty years she had been deprived of about a quarter of her civic population.

An additional symptom of degrading pauperism was the difficulty of coping with the expenses required for burial. In the *Ekklesiazousai* mention is made of people who do not own enough land for their graves.[34] This is not only a figure of speech, for in the *Ploutos* living a life of toil and dying without even leaving behind enough money for the funeral is regarded as one of the characteristic traits of poverty.[35] Moreover, in a speech which appears to have been composed at about the same date as Aristophanes' *Ploutos*, Lysias mentions the financing of funerals as one of the main forms of assistance that a wealthy man can offer needy fellow citizens.[36]

The connection between abject poverty and crime is emphasized in the contemporary or slightly later Greek literature, especially in the works of Plato and Aristotle. Plato remarks that "wherever you see beggars in a city, there are somewhere in the neighbourhood concealed thieves and cutpurses and temple robbers and similar experts in crime."[37] Later, Aristotle was to follow his master when stating that "poverty produces sedition and crime."[38]

The last extant plays of Aristophanes stress the connection between extreme poverty and crime, especially theft; they contain cumulative evidence of the existence of thieves and of the dimensions of the phenomenon in Athenian society of the fourth century. It is worth noting that many references are concerned with cloak thieves. Mention is made, for instance, of thieves who attack at night tearing the victim's clothes.[39] Praxagora tells her husband that she wore his shoes in order to look like a man and save, by her appearance, his overcloak from thieves ...[40] The problem of theft is certainly not confined to clothes but much more general. Mention is also made of temple robbers, house burglars and other sorts of artists in crime.[41] The variety of legal terms used for theft is

---

[33a] *Eccl.* 1132; cf. Plat. *Symp.* 175 E.

[34] *Eccl.* 592; cf. W. E. Heitland, *Agricola. A Study of Agriculture and Rustic Life* ... (Cambridge, 1921), p. 41: "Even a comic poet would hardly put this into the mouth of one of his characters if there were not some section of the audience to whom it might appeal".

[35] *Plut.* 555.

[36] Lys. 19, 59.

[37] *Resp.* 552 D; cf. *Leg.* 679B.

[38] *Pol.* 1265b 12: "ἡ δὲ πενία στάσιν ἐμποιεῖ καὶ κακουργίαν." cf. 1295b11; 1320a 32ff.: "the duty of a genuine democrat is to see that the masses are not extremely poor; for this is what causes democracy to be corrupt".

[39] *Eccl.* 668; cf. 565; *Av.* 496-8, and see next note.

[40] *Eccl.* 544f.; cf. Ussher, *Eccl.* p. 150 (*ad loc.*).

[41] *Plut.* 30; 165; 204-6; 357f.; 565; 869; cf. *Eccl.* 661.

noteworthy; not only *klopē* (just theft), but also *harpagē* (robbery with violence) and *aposterēsis* (embezzlement).[42]

After hearing the exposition of his wife's schemes, Blepyros cannot help asking her whether the new regime will do away with all thieves. Her answer is that these will disappear, since everybody will be provided with the necessities of life.[43] However, this argument had already met with Chremes' objection that prosperity had not actually stopped the wealthy stealing more and more; on the contrary, they had proved to be the biggest thieves.[44] This objection had been raised within the context of the discussion on Praxagora's proposals only a few lines before, but such arguments cannot shake the self-confidence of a committed revolutionary. Nevertheless, Aristophanes' objections to Praxagora's "communism" on this specific point as well as on others seem to have had a not inconsiderable influence on later criticism and refutation of "communist", collectivist, or egalitarian systems.

In his criticism of the theories of Phaleas the Chalkedonian,[45] Aristotle observes that it is not enough to equalize men's properties[46] unless a moderate size is prescribed for all,[47] and even that will not be sufficient unless the lawgiver is able to level men's desires. According to this view, egalitarianism does not take into account human passions and human corruption. Men do wrong not only for the sake of the bare necessities of life but also to gain pleasure and satisfy desire. Therefore, preventing

---

[42] For κλοπή; ἁρπαγή and ἀποστέρησις, see *Plut.* 372-3.

[43] *Eccl.* 667-9.

[44] *Eccl.* 608; cf. Ussher, *Eccl.* p. 160 (*ad loc.*). "His (viz., Aristophanes') reference is not made more specific, but he no doubt has in mind the leading public figures in the city". Ussher points out several references to embezzlement by politicians from public funds (*Vesp.* 663ff.; 1100; *Plut.* 569) and compares with Xen. *Anab.* 4, 6, 16, where the Athenians, particularly their leaders, are said to have been known as clever at stealing public funds. For further evidence, see below, n. 71. However, Chremes' statement is of a general impact, and there is no reason to reduce its scope only to leading public figures, as Ussher has done.

[45] *Pol.* 1266a 39ff.; On Phaleas, see W. L. Newman, *The Politics of Aristotle* II (Oxford, 1887), p. 283ff.; E. Barker, *Greek Political Theory. Plato and his Predecessors*[5] (repr., 1964), p. 92f.; R. von Pöhlmann, *Geschichte der sozialen Frage und des Sozialismus in der antiken Welt*[3] II (1925), p. 5ff.; I. Lana, "Le teorie egalitarie di Falea di Calcedone", *Rivista critica di storia della filosofia* (1950), p. 265ff.

[46] Even with regard to properties, Aristotle wondered why Phaleas had taken care to secure equality in land only and left other forms of wealth untouched. (*Pol.* 1267b9ff.) This remark is highly reminiscent of Chremes' question in *Eccl.* 601-2: "What about those who do not possess land, but silver and Darics (of gold), that is non-apparent wealth (ἀφανῆ πλοῦτον)?"

[47] If not, equality of properties may exist, but their size may be either unduly large and promote luxury or unduly small, causing penury (*Pol.* 1266b24ff.). The middle way recommended by Aristotle reminds us not only of Plato's *Laws*—to which the *Politics* has striking affinities—but also of Aristophanes' economic ideal. See also below, p. 38ff. and n. 206.

highway robbery by removing the problems of hunger and cold, cannot, in Aristotle's opinion, be a panacea for social ills.[48]

It is hard not to see the probability of Aristophanes' influence on Aristotle's critical remarks regarding this particular issue as well as others. When presenting, within the context of his criticism of Plato's *Republic*, the impracticability of "communism" from the psychological point of view, Aristotle seems to be inspired to a considerable extent by Aristophanes.[49] The philosopher's argument that more quarrels will occur among those possessing or using property in common than among those who possess their own estates[50] reminds us of the citizen who, in the *Ekklesiazousai*, tries to find a way of keeping his own property without forfeiting his share in the benefits distributed by the new regime. Among other arguments for not giving up his private property, this citizen mentions the fickleness of the Athenian citizens, who are easily persuaded to vote in their Assembly and then, after voting in hot haste, they refuse to carry out their resolutions.[51] This is one of the many examples showing Aristophanes' ability to mingle political and social aspects.

However, the main purpose of the long scene presenting the confrontation of the anonymous citizen with Chremes is to reflect the psychological inhibitions of the average man when required to renounce his private property. The attempts to identify this citizen[52] seem not only to be futile, but also to miss the main point, since it is his anonymity, not his identity, which is significant. Despite the warnings not to take Aristophanes too seriously[53] on this point as well as on others, the comic

---

[48] *Pol.* 1267 a 2ff. See esp. 1267 a 12f.: "The greatest crimes are committed for the sake of superfluities, not for the sake of necessities". This remark looks almost like a prose paraphrase of Chremes' words in *Eccl.* 608.

[49] This does not imply the acceptance of the view advocating that Aristophanes was satirizing Plato's *Republic* in the *Ekklesiazousai*; for, as we shall try to show later, this view is hardly acceptable.

[50] *Pol.* 1263b23ff.; cf. 1262b37ff., esp. 63a17ff.

[51] *Eccl.* 797-8 and 812ff.; see also below, n. 158. This is reminiscent of Kleon's complaints against the attempt to revoke the decision on the fate of the Mytileneans only a day after it had been voted (Thuc. 3, 37-40).

[52] See Ussher, *Eccl.* p. 181.

[53] See esp. *ibid.*: "But we must not see him (viz., the anonymous citizen) as a peg to hang a thesis on: Aristophanes does *not* (Ussher's italics) mean that plans for common ownership will founder through individuals' greed"; cf. Ussher's general view of the play (above, n. 1); cf. *ibid.* p. XXX: "He does not present it (viz., the communistic programme) as a serious solution, nor does he, on the other hand condemn it ... Aristophanes is playing for the laughs. This is a simple truth ..." (see also above, n. 1). I refuse to believe that the truth is so simple. With respect to Aristophanes' alleged lack of seriousness, it is worth quoting a remark made by W. G. Forrest in his criticism of A. W. Gomme's view that Aristophanes was not commenting seriously on politics but was just making jokes. ("Aristophanes and Politics", *CR* 52 (1938), p. 97ff., repr. in *More Essays in Greek History and Literature* (Oxford, 1962), p. 70ff.). Forrest rightly objects that "from the

poet is here offering his audience, by the means appropriate to his *genre*, a personal opinion on the impracticability of "communism",[54] and his view is reminiscent of the argument Aristotle was later to advance on the ideas advocating the suppression of man's natural inclination towards the private ownership of property. Both Aristophanes and Aristotle strongly disapprove also of the abolition of the family, although, for obvious reasons, they express their views in different ways, as befits their different *genres*. In Aristophanes the rejection of sexual "communism" is not given a detailed, theoretical justification. It is prepared by the very way the ideas are exposed by Praxagora, as well as by her interlocutors' questions within the *agōn* as, for instance, "But how are any of us going to recognize our own children?"[55] Later on, the refutation of the heroine's schemes is further elaborated by their grotesque appearance when put into practice.

3. *Poverty versus Riches*

Up to this point our discussion has mainly stressed certain aspects of poverty as presented in Aristophanes' last extant plays. However, it is

---

fact that someone is not commenting seriously it does not follow that he is not commenting with serious intentions". ("Aristophanes and the Athenian Empire", in B. Levick, ed., *The Ancient Historian and his Materials. Essays in Honour of C. E. Stevens on his Seventieth Birthday* (Farnborough, 1975), p. 18). Although Gomme and Forrest do not deal with the *Ekklesiazousai*, both the attitude of Gomme and the criticism of Forrest are significant to our context. See also the criticism of Gomme by G. E. M. de Ste. Croix, *The Origins of the Peloponnesian War* (London, 1972), App. XXIX, p. 355ff., whose remarks are very useful for an historical approach to Aristophanic comedy.

[54] Cf. Couat, *Aristophane*, p. 205f.; E. Roos, "De exodi Ecclesiazusarum fabulae ratione et consilio", *Eranos* 49 (1951), p. 5ff.; 15. See also above, n. 46.

[55] *Eccl.* 635ff.; cf. Arist. *Pol.* 1262a 10ff. The question "how will a father recognize his children" is also raised by Glaukon in Plato's *Republic* (461 C): "... how are they to distinguish one another's fathers and daughters and the other relations that you have just mentioned?" The answer is similar to that given by Praxagora. She affirms that "the children will regard all older men as fathers"; cf. Sokrates' answer in *Resp.* 461D: all children born in the tenth or seventh month after the "wedding" will be regarded by him as sons or daughters ... Similarly all children born in the period in which their fathers and mothers were procreating will regard one another as brothers and sisters. This will suffice to avoid incest. However, Aristotle was not convinced by these arguments: on the one hand he argues that family likeness will in many cases indicate parentage (*Pol.* 1262a 14ff.); on the other hand he points to the high risk of incest (*ibid.* 32ff.). Another problem which arises in connection with sexual "communism" is that of assaults on parents. Praxagora dismisses the danger saying that under the new regime if someone is getting beaten up, many will rush to help him thinking that he may be their father. (*Eccl.* 637-42). Again, there is a significant similarity with Plato's argument (*Resp.* 465 A): a young man will not dare to strike an elder, so as not to lay hands on a man who may be his father and also out of fear that other citizens will rush to the aid of the victim thinking that he may be their father, brother or son. These arguments could not convince Aristotle that assaults on parents will not frequently occur under sexual "communism". (*Pol.* 1262a 25ff.).

impossible fully to understand this problem and the crisis in Athenian society as depicted by the playwright without a proper examination of the basic socio-economic contrast, that of poverty versus riches, which is at the very core of the social conflict.

From this viewpoint it is worth quoting Chremylos' statement in the *Ploutos*: "Our life nowadays can only be described as madness or lunacy. For many wicked men are rich having amassed wealth unjustly, while many others though scrupulously honest are poor and hungry, and live mostly with you" (viz. Poverty).[56] It is important to stress that Zeus is blamed for the present situation of mankind: he is accused of having immorally blinded Ploutos out of caprice and ill-will to men.[57] The antagonism between rich and poor is repeatedly emphasized in Aristophanes' last extant plays especially from a moral point of view, i.e., wicked rich versus honest poor.

This does not mean that Aristophanes is no longer interested in certain political aspects of the socio-economic conflict, for he still is. The audience is told, for instance, that whenever a motion proposing new ships for the navy is introduced, the poor citizens vote in its favour, whereas the rich and the farmers oppose it.[58] The urban poor were interested in earning a living by serving in the navy.[59] The rich citizens were afraid of the trierarchy imposed on them, which compelled them to finance the maintenance and repair of the triremes.[60] The farmers were naturally hostile to military service and were economically affected by the war more than the townsmen, particularly if the war was accompanied by inroads on their lands.[61] This explains their coalition with the rich on this issue now, as in the past, during the Peloponnesian War.[62]

---

[56] *Plut.* 500-4.

[57] *Plut.* 87-92; cf. Ehrenberg, *The People of Aristophanes*, p. 71: "However, when Zeus, who made Ploutos blind, is said to have profited by his blindness, the joke ceases to be harmless and becomes very bitter". On Aristophanes' attitude towards the gods, see also below, esp. nn. 139; 172.

[58] *Eccl.* 197-8; cf. Ussher, *Eccl.* p. 102 (*ad loc.*).

[59] Cf. *Plut.* 172. Formerly, before the defeat of 404 B.C., they had been interested also in other benefits which they could enjoy thanks to Athens' thalassocracy, especially allotments in cleruchies and the elaborate system of *misthophoria* (cf. Ps.-Xen. *Ath. Pol.* 1, 16).

[60] See, e.g., Aristoph. *Eq.* 912; Ps.-Xen. *Ath. Pol.* 1, 13; Lys. 21, 2; 6; 32, 26-27.

[61] See, e.g., Aristoph. *Ach.* 183; *Pax*, 628; cf Ehrenberg, *The People of Aristophanes*, p. 50; 81f.

[62] Cf. Ps.-Xen. *Ath. Pol.* 2, 14; the Old Oligarch presents the same antagonism of interests as found in the *Eccl.* 197-8, i.e., between the farmers and the wealthy on the one hand, and the poor (whom he calls the *dēmos*) on the other hand; cf. *Hell. Oxy.* 1, 2-3. On the connection between thalassocracy and democracy see also, e.g., Ps.-Xen. *Ath. Pol.* 1, 2; 14-20; Plat. *Leg.* 704A-705A; Arist. *Ath. Pol.* 27, 1.

However, this old motif of Aristophanic comedy is only mentioned *en passant* in the *Ekklesiazousai*. In his last plays the comic poet is more interested in the general antagonism between rich and poor, regardless of whether the economic sector they belong to is urban or agrarian, even if he still feels a special sympathy for the poor among the farmers.

The debt problem, which is organically connected with the situation of poverty versus riches, is emphasized in Aristophanes' last plays as well as in contemporary or slightly later literature.[63]

Praxagora stresses that under the new regime there will be "no more harrying for debt."[64] Later, when asked about the payment of fines in cases of legal action, her prompt answer is that there will be no more lawsuits.[65] Her interlocutors can hardly believe this, and Blepyros asks what will happen if a debtor refuses to repay a debt. Praxagora's answer is that the creditor will be suspected of theft, since everything, including money, is to be held in common.[66] Hence, the disappearance of the debt problem is regarded as one of the principal blessings of the new regime.

In the *Ploutos*, Karion is said to have been enslaved because he had not paid a small debt.[67] He could not have been enslaved in Athens, where servitude for debts had been abolished a long time before by Solon. Karion must have been enslaved in his own state (unknown to us) and later bought by Chremylos. It is important to note that references to enslavement of Greeks as a result of debt-contracts (and for trifling sums) occur in comtemporary literature.[68] When Aristophanes ascribed to Chremylos the Panhellenic intention of expelling Poverty from Hellas[69] (not only from Athens), he probably had in mind, among other things, the problem of debt-slaves. That Chremylos himself enjoyed the services of such a slave may be an element of dramatic irony.

---

[63] See, e.g., Plat. *Resp.* 549E-552A; 555C-E; Plato's view was that the dangers of money-lending should be solved by the device of denying legal protection to the creditors (See *ibid.* 556A-B; *Leg.* 742C). See also Isocr. *Panath.* 259 (*chreōn apokopai*); cf. Fuks, "Patterns and Types of Revolution" (above, n. 3), p. 54f.; 65; 69; 77.

[64] *Eccl.* 567: I prefer this translation of "μὴ 'νεχυραζόμενον φέρειν". Another possibility is "no distraining on your goods" (Rogers, *Aristophanes* III (London, Loeb, 1924), p. 297; cf. Ussher, *Eccl.* p. 153 (*ad loc.*), who points out both possibilities and rightly remarks that the difference is not of much importance since anyway debts are to disappear.

[65] *Eccl.* 655-58; cf. 561: "no more witnessing, no more informing", and see below, the discussion dealing with the sycophant in the *Ploutos*; cf. Plat. *Resp.* 464D: "There will be no lawsuits (δίκαι) and accusations (ἐγκλήματα) against one another". Once more Aristotle was not persuaded by the argument (*Pol.* 1263b 15ff.).

[66] *Eccl.* 659-61.

[67] *Plut.* 147-8: "... διὰ μικρὸν ἀργυρίδιον δοῦλος γεγένημαι". Cf. ll. 6-7.

[68] Lys. 12 (*in Eratosth.*), 98; Isocr. *Plat.* 48. In both cases mention is made of enslavement due to petty debts (μικρῶν ἕνεκα συμβολαίων); cf. Ehrenberg, *The People of Aristophanes*, p. 169.

[69] *Plut.* 464.

The wealthy are severely censured, both in the *Ekklesiazousai* and in the *Ploutos*, especially in the latter, for their evil ways, arrogance, physical degeneration, effeminacy, breaking of laws, cowardliness, laziness and other vices.[70] Therefore, to argue that "Aristophanes scarcely says a disrespectful word about the rich as such"[70a] equates with making a grave error of judgement. The sharpest arrows are aimed at the *nouveaux riches*. The censure of these is not a new motif in Attic comedy. Aristophanes seems to have fully developed, in his last comedies, a social motif already existent in his *genre*,[71] and to have pushed the attacks on the newly rich to the extreme: "they place no limit to their villainy"; "every single one amongst them is bad"[72] (this is stated by Wealth himself!); the only way to succeed in life seems to be by becoming a criminal or a villain[73] (Chremylos' words); "as soon as they (viz. the orators) have enriched themselves at public expense, they become criminals; they plot against the masses and make war against the people"[74] (Poverty's state-

---

[70] *Eccl.* 424; 567; 608; *Plut.* 30-1; 49-50; 202; 237-8; 342; 502-3; 559-60; 564; 588-9; 754-5; Plat. *Resp.* 421E-422A; 550E; 555C-D; 556B-D; *Leg.* 742E; 869E-870A; see Fuks, "The Conditions of 'Riches' and of 'Poverty' in Plato's *Republic*", *RSA* 6/7 (1976/77), p. 65ff.

[70a] Ste. Croix, *The Origins of the Peloponnesian War*, p. 360. Here the author tries "to discover, by way of contrast, who is that emerges with credit from the plays of Aristophanes". To be on the safe, he admits that "in the *Plutus*, the nature of the plot is such that occasional unflattering references to the rich are bound to occur, but even here they are a few ... and esp. referring to the orators". This argument is hardly acceptable in view of the passages cited in the previous note.

[71] Kratinos, for instance, had contrasted the "rich man of olden times" (ἀρχαιόπλουτος ἐξ ἀρχῆς; D. L. Page, *Greek Literary Papyri* I (London, Loeb, 1942) F 38 b 32) with the "rascally new rich" (νεοπλουτοπόνηρος—Kock, I, fr. 208). Krates spoke of the man who had become rich through wrong-doing (ἀδικοχρήματος—Kock, I, fr. 42); cf. R. Goossens, "Les *Ploutoi* de Kratinos", *REA* 37 (1935), p. 412; 425; Ehrenberg, *The People of Aristophanes*, p. 239ff.; id. "Pericles and his Colleagues", *AJP* 66 (1945), p. 120, n. 23.

[72] *Plut.* 108-11.

[73] *Plut.* 37-8.

[74] *Plut.* 567-70; cf. 379, and see the examples of Pamphilos (ll. 174-5) and Neokleides (below, n. 186). Enrichment at the public expense, i.e., embezzlement of public funds and bribery are not new motifs in Aristophanes' last plays. See, e.g., *Eq.* 402-4; 438; 472-3; 680-2; 834-5; 1359-60; *Nub.* 591; *Vesp.* 675-7; *Ran.* 360ff.; *Thesm.* 946-7; cf. Kock, I, fr. 100; 219, and see also Kratinos, *loc. cit.* (above, n. 71), who seems to have played with the double meaning of ἐξ ἀρχῆς (i.e., "from the start" and "from office"). It is particularly important to pay attention to the contemporary evidence provided by Lysias' speech *Against Ergokles* (XXVIII), which was delivered in 388 B.C., the very year of the *Ploutos*' production. All the speech is relevant to our issue, but particularly the passage alleging that as soon as the *stratēgoi* get rich, they regard themselves as alien to the city, and even hate its people; they plan to become its rulers instead of being its subjects (28, 6-7). See also *id.* 27 (*in Epicr.*), *passim*, a speech delivered about 390 B.C. against an important Treasury official, a man of wealth and influence (and a good orator), accused of having embezzled public funds and of having taken bribes (cf. *Hell. Oxy.* 2, 2; Paus. 3, 9, 8). He is mentioned by Aristophanes in *Eccl.* 71; cf. Ussher, p. XXII and p. 84. (See also Plat. *Gorg.* 525D-526B; here it is possible to find the idea that politicians are amongst the

ment, fully accepted by Chremylos and his friend); those who grow rich and prosper are "temple breakers, orators, informers and knaves."[75] (Chremylos' words).

It is important to stress that the attacks on the wealthy do not represent the particular point of view of only one character, but are repeatedly uttered by various *dramatis personae*, who otherwise are antagonists. Not only Penia has hard words to say about the rich but also Chremylos, and even Ploutos. The single point on which Penia's interlocutors can completely confirm the truth of her words, despite their hatred for her, is her description of the politicians who had enriched themselves at public expense. And Poverty's words are strikingly similar to those of Wealth in this respect, although those of the latter were even more general, referring to the whole group of the *nouveaux riches*. All in all, the point of view can certainly be established as that of the playwright. Moreover, Aristophanes expects his audience to identify with these statements, in which case they can be taken as irrefutable evidence for the intensity of hostility which many Athenians felt for the wealthy, particularly for the newly rich. They appear to be *a priori* suspected of having made their fortune by unsavoury methods.[76] Amongst the most outspoken suspects were the corn merchants, some of whom had succeeded in making a considerable fortune. Aristophanes mentions this group in connection with Blepyros' proposal[77] and provides us with the name of one of its prominent members—Nausikydes,[78] who does not seem to have been particularly popular in Athens.[79]

---

greatest criminals; an honest politician is a remarkable exception. The *Gorgias* was probably composed around 395 B.C.; see A. E. Taylor, *Plato. The Man and his Work*, p. 103f, n. 1.) On Epikrates, cf. J. K. Davies, *Athenian Propertied Families* (Oxford, 1971), p. 181.

[75] *Plut.* 30-1: "ἱερόσυλοι, ῥήτορες, συχοφάνται καὶ πονηροί". The inclusion of the orators (i.e., politicians) in this list is highly significant: see previous note; on Aristophanes' attitude towards sycophants, see the discussion below and especially n. 183.

[76] See, e.g., *Plut.* 502; 754-5 and *passim*. Particularly important from this viewpoint is the scene in which Blepsidemos refuses to believe that his friend, Chremylos, could have made a fortune by honest means: see *Plut.* 335-90; cf. Q. Cataudella, "Due note ad Aristofane", *Athen.* 13 (1935), p. 203: "Blessidemo ... osserva che l'arrichire improvvisamente ... non è cosa di uomo che abbia commesso azione onesta". Cataudella compares this remark with Anon. Iamb. (see in H. Diels-W. Kranz, *Die Fragmente der Vorsokratiker* II⁶ (Berlin, 1952), 89, 2, 8.

[77] See above, n. 10.

[78] *Eccl.* 426; cf. Xen. *Mem.* 2, 7, 6, where it is stated that Nausikydes had amassed a fortune from his business in grain (ἀπ' ἀλφιτοποιίας). Hence he became one of the richest citizens and often had to undertake *leitourgiai*.

[79] In spite of the costly public services he had to finance. The general attitude towards him is obvious from the comment Blepyros added to his proposal: "That good, at least, they (viz., the poor) would have gained from Nausikydes". (*ibid.*); cf. Rogers, *Eccl.* p. 66 (*ad loc.*): "it is natural that a man who had acquired such great riches in such a trade should be accused, whether justly or unjustly, of having made his money by harsh and

In his speech *Against the Corn Dealers* (386 B.C.), Lysias provides evidence of the hatred towards this group in contemporary Athens. He compares the grain merchants to enemies who besiege the city in time of peace.[80] Mention is made of great numbers in this trade who have been tried for their lives; it is stated that they prefer to risk death every day rather than cease making illicit gains.[81] In the speech *Against Epikrates* (delivered about 390 B.C., during the Corinthian War), Lysias mentions war-profiteers, *nouveaux riches* who made a fortune at the expense of the people; these are presented as thieves.[82]

Later Isokrates was to comment, in the *Antidosis*, on the change which had come over Athens during his life-time: "For even when I was a boy, wealth was regarded as so secure as well as admirable that almost everyone affected to own more property than he actually possessed because he wanted to enjoy the standing which it gave. Now, on the other hand, a man has to be ready to defend himself for being rich as if it were the worst of crimes, and to keep on the alert if he is to avoid disaster; for it has become far more dangerous to be suspected of being well-off than to be detected in crime."[83] In order to defend themselves against such suspicions, the wealthy sometimes tried to prove, by means of *euergesia* (good service, especially through financial contributions) that they were useful (*chrēstoi*) to the *polis*.[84] This was far from being a satisfactory solution to the social conflict. Moreover, the *euergesia* could be considered as additional grounds for suspicion.[85]

The tension between the poor and the rich, and the deep animosity between the masses and the well-to-do, are widespread motifs in the Greek literature of the fourth century. Plato summed up the gravity of the crisis in his famous dictum about the collapse of unity in the state, which is no more "one, but two states, the one of poor, the other of rich men; they are living on the same spot but always conspiring against one

---

ungenerous dealing: and that is the innuendo in the line before us." See also Van Daele, *Aristophane* V (Budé), p. 34, n. 1: "Ces profiteurs de la misère publique réalisaient d'énormes bénéfices."

[80] Lys. 22, 15.

[81] *Ibid.* 20; cf. also *ibid.* 13.

[82] *Id.* 27, 10-11.

[83] Isocr. *Antid.* 159-160; cf. A. Fuks, "Isokrates and the Social-Economic Situation in Greece", *Anc. Soc.* 3 (1972), p. 22f.

[84] See, e.g., Lys. 24, 17: "The wealthy purchase with their money escape from the risk that they run"; cf. *id.* 19, 59; 21, 12; 15; cf. Anon. Iamb. in Diels-Kranz, II⁶, 89, 3, 3-4. See esp. E. Lévy, *Athènes devant la défaite de 404. Histoire d'une crise idéologique*, Bibliothèque des Écoles Françaises d'Athènes et de Rome, 225 (1976), p. 243ff.; 250: "L'évergétisme était un moyen pour les riches de se faire pardonner leur richesse".

[85] See, e.g., Lys. 27, 11; cf. *Plut.* 335-90.

another.''[86] In the oration *Archidamos* (around 366 B.C.), Isokrates states that the Greeks fear their fellow citizens more than they fear the enemy: ''the well-to-do had rather throw their possessions into the sea than help the needy'', whereas the poor ''would less gladly discover a treasure than seize the possessions of the wealthy.''[87]

To return to Aristophanes, the proposals of Euaion, Blepyros[88] and, what is most important, Praxagora's programme, are motivated and determined not only by poverty *per se* but also, perhaps even mainly, by the situation of poverty versus riches. Praxagora stresses that the new regime, based on equality, means the abolition of the present social order of abject poverty and extreme wealth: ''All things are to be held in common and belong to everybody; all shall live by that; there shall be no rich, no poor; no great landowner and another who has not enough land to be buried in; no one shall possess a plenty of servants while another has none; all shall have one common and equal system of life.''[89]

4. *The Sources of the ''Communistic'' Ideas*

The most controversial problem concerning the *Ekklesiazousai* is the origin of the ideas parodied by Aristophanes in the play. Many scholars have pointed out the existence of similarities between the ''communism'' envisaged by Aristophanes' heroine and certain ideas of Plato's *Republic*, such as community of property, women and children, the ensuing absence of lawsuits and the establishment of common messes.[90] Consequently some of these scholars have tried to interpret the attested

---

[86] *Resp.* 551D; see also, e.g., 422E-423A; 552C; E; 555D-E; 556C-E; 564B; D-E; 565A-C; 565E-566A; 566C and *passim*. The last paragraph is particularly important since it assumes that the man who has wealth is regarded as an enemy of the people (μισόδημος); cf. Lys. *locc. citt.* in nn. 80 and 82 above and Isocr. *loc. cit.* in n. 83 above, and see next note. On the problem of poverty versus riches in Plato's *Republic*, see A. Fuks, ''The Conditions of 'Riches' and of 'Poverty' in Plato's *Republic*'' (above, n. 70), p. 63ff.; *id.* ''Plato and the Social Question: The Problem of Poverty and Riches in the *Republic*'', *Anc. Soc.* 8 (1977), p. 49ff. On the same problem in Plato's *Laws*, see *id. Anc. Soc.* 10 (1979), p. 33ff.

[87] Isocr. *Archid.* 67. This statement of Isokrates was particularly influenced by the outburst of revolutionary agitation in the Peloponnese after the Spartan defeat at Leuktra (371 B.C.). Nevertheless, the problem of poverty versus riches had been present in Isokrates' consciousness a long time before, ever since the composition of the *Panegyrikos* (about 380 B.C.). See Fuks, ''Isokrates'' (above, n. 76), p. 18ff.; 33ff., with copious evidence.

[88] See above, nn. 10 and 30.

[89] *Eccl.* 590-4.

[90] For community of property, women and children and the absence of lawsuits, see above, nn. 55 and 65. On the establishment of common messes, see below, nn. 116, 123. For a detailed analysis of the specific parallels, see J. Adam, *The Republic of Plato*[2] I (Cambridge, 1963), p. 350ff. and Ussher, *Eccl.* p. 157ff. One has, however, to be careful not to exaggerate the similarities: see the discussion below.

similarities by regarding the play as a satire at the expense of Plato's views.[91]

This theory is untenable for many reasons. First of all it would meet the obvious difficulty of chronology, since the *Republic* was composed almost twenty years after the play.[92] To solve the problem of such an anticipated satire, it has been suggested that Plato had begun to expose his ideal State to his disciples a long time before the final writing, and, therefore, Aristophanes and others could have been familiar with either an early, oral, version of the *Republic* or with a first section of this work.[93] In view of the lack of any factual basis, this view must remain, at best, purely hypothetical, and even as such it encounters serious difficulties.

In the play Aristophanes was reacting to ideas which ought to have been familiar to the large Athenian public; otherwise the audience would not have been in a position to understand the parody and the satire. However, Plato's ideas, even when written in their final form, do not seem to have belonged to the genre of literature which attracts the attention of the public at large. It is even less plausible that the Athenian audience would have been familiar with Plato's ideas from a yet uncompleted manuscript or from preliminary exposition and discussion amongst a narrow circle of disciples and friends. One should add that Aristophanes would have had no particular reason not to mention Plato

---

[91] See, e.g., Rogers, *Eccl.* p. XXIIf.; G. Norwood, *Greek Comedy* (London, 1931), p. 269; G. Nicosia, *Economia e Politica di Atene attraverso Aristofane* (Milano, 1935), p. 81; Murray, *Aristophanes*, p. 187ff.; cf. J. Luccioni, *La pensée politique de Platon* (Paris, 1958), p. 298; cf. more recently Lévy, *Athènes devant la défaite* (above, n. 84), p. 208, who is inconclusive on this issue: "... que Platon soit réellment à la source de ces conceptions ou qu'il se soit contenté de les reprendre ..."; cf. D. Barrett in Aristophanes, *The Knights and Other Plays* (Harmondsworth, Penguin, 1978), Intr. to the *Assemblywomen*, p. 218; T. B. L. Webster, *Studies in Later Greek Comedy²* (Manchester, 1970), p. 34f.; Th. M. de Wit-Tak, Review of Ussher, *Aristoph. Eccl.*, *Mnemosyne* 30 (1977), p. 83f. For a detailed survey of older literature, see Adam, *ibid.* p. 345ff.

[92] The almost commonly accepted view ascribes the date of the *Republic* to the mid-seventies of the fourth century. See e.g., A. Diès, *Platon, La République* (Paris, Budé, 1947), p. XCIVff., with a summary of older literature; cf. G. C. Field, *Plato and his Contemporaries³* (London, 1967), p. 70f. and esp. Fuks, "Plato and the Social Question" (above, n. 86), p. 51f., with further literature.

[93] See esp. A. Chiapelli, "Le *Ecclesiazusae* di Aristofane e la *Repubblica* di Platone", *Riv. Fil.* 11 (1883), p. 209; Norwood, *loc. cit.* (above, n. 91); Luccioni, *loc. cit.* (above, n. 91); cf. Rogers, *loc. cit.* (above, n. 91) and M. Pohlenz, *Aus Platos Werdezeit* (Berlin, 1913), p. 227ff., who assume an early edition. It has even been argued that the recapitulation of the *Republic* in the *Timaios* (17Cff.) was based on a preliminary draft of the dialogue or on its first part (Usener, as quoted by Adam, *op. cit.* p. 353f.), a thesis which seems to have no solid basis. For the criticism of these views see, e.g., Wilamowitz, *Lysistrate*, p. 204 and n. 1; Field, *op. cit.* p. 59 and n. 1; W. J. W. Koster, *Naar Aanleiding van het Communisme bij Aristophanes en Plato* (Groningen, 1955), p. 7ff.; Dover, *Aristophanic Comedy*, p. 200f.; Fuks, "Patterns and Types of Revolution" (above, n. 3), p. 62, n. 14.

within his play had he really been the target of his comic arrows; this silence is hardly compatible with Aristophanes' comic methods.[94]

Furthermore, Plato's "communism", despite the attested similarities, is vastly different from that exposed and mocked in the play. It is aristocratic, elitist and austere, whereas Praxagora's is democratic, vulgar and extremely hedonistic. Plato's "communism" is motivated by the desire to neutralize the materialistic tendencies of society, whereas Praxagora's encourages them. The abolition of the family by Praxagora is presented chiefly as a means to achieve equality between citizens, men and women, in the satisfaction of sexual desires, not as a device for achieving social unity, as it is in Plato's *Republic* (with regard to the first two classes, of course). All this stresses the implausibility of the theory which sees the origin of Praxagora's ideas in Plato.[95]

Certain scholars have advanced the view that both Aristophanes and Plato were inspired by a common philosophical source, and several possibilities have been raised as to the identity of that source, including the hypothesis of a work written by Protagoras or Antisthenes, which has not survived.[96] However, most of the difficulties raised above remain unsolved by this theory: the silence of Aristophanes regarding that source, to which we now have to add, in this case, Plato's silence; the improbability that a large section of the Athenian audience would have been familiar with such a work; the profound dissimilarities between Praxagora's ideas and Plato's. To these difficulties we have to add the

---

[94] The argument that they were friends, advanced by Murray (*Aristophanes*, p. 188), is not convincing. See Ussher, *Eccl.* p. xvi, n. 7, where he also rightly rejects the argument of G. Zuccante ("Aristofane e Platone", *RIL* 62 (1929), p. 380; 385) about the limitation of personal invective in Athens by the decree of Syrakosios. See also M. Radin, "Freedom of Speech in Ancient Athens", *AJP* 48 (1927), p. 219ff. It is obvious that the last plays of Aristophanes contain many violent attacks on contemporaries. The attempt to identify one of these figures, Aristyllos (*Eccl.* 647; *Plut.* 314), as Plato—on the premise that the name was a diminutive for Aristokles and that the latter was Plato's real name—is ingenious yet hardly acceptable (The attempt was first made by Bergk, *Comment. de rel. com. Attic. antiq.* (1838), p. 403, and later accepted by other scholars, e.g., Norwood, *Greek Comedy*, p. 265). But see the just criticism of Adam, *Republic*, p. 348: "If Plato is personated by Aristyllus, we can only say that his features are distorted beyond the possibility of recognition ... nor is it likely that Aristophanes, even in a late comedy ... would have had recourse to so far-fetched a cryptogram."

[95] Cf. Croiset, *Aristophanes*, p. 173ff.

[96] The view advocating Protagoras as the common source is mainly based on the assertion of Aristoxenos and Favorinus (*ap.* Diog. Laert. 3, 37; 57) that Plato's *Republic* was found almost entirely in Protagoras' *Antilogika*; cf. Porphyrion in Diels-Kranz, II, 264, 12. See Adam, *op. cit.* p. 352 who makes the suggestion and then rightly rejects it on the spot; cf. Ussher, *Eccl.* p. XIXf., with a summary of the literature. Ussher mentions also the theory that Antisthenes was the common predecessor (*ibid.* p. XX, n. 4). He favours in principle the view that an earlier philosopher was the common source, but admits that "in our present state of knowledge any answer will be tentative."

authority of Aristotle, who showed a vivid interest in philosophical treatises concerned with "communist" ideas. Within the context of his discussion of such ideas he remarks that his master was the first (meaning the first philosopher) to have proposed community of women and children.[97]

Finally, it is worth stressing that Aristophanes himself does not make even the slightest allusion suggesting that the ideas were connected with the work of a philosopher, or, in fact, of any particular person.

The most plausible source of the proposals raised in the *Ekklesiazousai* is to be found in ideas which were "in the air" at that time. Some of these ideas were more practical and of limited scope, like those parodied in the proposals put into the mouth of Euaion and Blepyros; other ideas were more radical and of a larger scope, like Praxagora's. We cannot know if the latter had already taken the shape of what is called utopia, but at least raw material, even if in a nebulous form, for the creation of this *genre* seems to have been in existence.[98]

During the last years of the Peloponnesian War and in the post-war generation, there was a perpetual search for a proper solution to the political or socio-economic crisis. Salvation (*sōtēria*) was a catchword in the political lexicon of the time.[99] The idea of salvation occupies a central place in Aristophanes' comedies. In his earlier plays he had particularly stressed the need of salvation from war or irresponsible and greedy demagogues. This meaning is also found at times in his last plays,[100] but the central aspect at this stage is socio-economic: salvation from the conditions of poverty.

It is worth stressing that, in the *Ekklesiazousai*, the Assembly of the people which decided to found a gynaecocracy had been faced with the ques-

---

[97] *Pol.* 1266a 34; cf. *ibid.* 74b 9-11; see Newman, *The Politics of Aristotle*, II, p. 282.

[98] Some scholars seem to have taken too extreme an approach when speaking of existing utopias; see, e.g., Ehrenberg, *The People of Aristophanes*, p. 67f. "... Utopias were undoubtedly in fashion ..."; cf. Vidal-Naquet, *op. cit.* (above, n. 4), p. 63ff.; Lévy, *Athènes devant la défaite*, p. 24; 207f. On the other hand, see the more careful approach of A. Fuks in his concise treatment of Aristophanes' last plays—"Patterns and Types of Revolution" (above, n. 3), p. 62: "... the ideas themselves are not, as is commonly supposed, rooted in philosophical or folk Utopianism, but in yearnings, schemes, proposals mooted in Athens in the 'nineties'."

[99] The catchword had frequently been used by oligarchic circles, especially on the eve of the two oligarchic revolutions (of 411 and 404/3 B.C.); see, e.g., Thuc. 8, 53, 2-3; 54, 1; Arist. *Ath. Pol.* 29, 2, 4, Lys. 12 (*in Eratosth.*), 68f.; 74. After the failure of these revolutions and Athens' defeat, the catchword was adopted by democratic propaganda; see, e.g., Lys. *ibid.* 26; 31; 50; 68f.; 85f.; 88; 98; see also *id.* 14, 10; 28, 15; cf. *id.* 2 (*Epitaph.*), 58; 64; 66; 68; Andoc. 3 (*Pax*), 12. See Lévy, *op. cit.* p. 16ff.; 23f.

[100] For the *sōtēria* motif in earlier plays of Aristophanes, see *Eq.* 149; 458; *Pax*, 301; 692; 867; 914; 1035-6; *Av.* 545; *Lys.* 29-30; 41; 525 and cp. with, e.g., *Eccl.* 202; 209; 234; see also V. Frey, "Zur Komödie des Aristophanes", *MH* 5 (1948), p. 169ff.

tion how to save the state, and that those who brought forward proposals presented themselves as saviours.[101]

In the *Ploutos*, the meaning of salvation has at times a broader impact, i.e., Panhellenic and even universal: not only Athens, but the whole of Greece, even all mankind, are to be saved from poverty. However, Athens remains the centre of Aristophanes' interest.[102]

References to Zeus the Saviour, frequently occur both in the *Ekklesiazousai* and in the *Ploutos*.[103] In the *Ploutos*, they contain a bitter irony and sarcasm since it is the same Zeus who is blamed for the actual condition of mankind.[104] After all, *sōtēria*, in the *Ploutos*, finally brings about the dethronement of Zeus Sōtēr. Chremylos and his friends are called "saviours of the god", i.e., of Ploutos, because they are going to save him from the blindness inflicted upon him by Zeus the Saviour,[105] and by saving him, save themselves. In other words, mankind has to be saved from its "Saviour". The last scene of the play significantly presents the priest of Zeus the Saviour, who, under the pressure of hunger decides to desert his master and stay with the saviours of Ploutos. To his surprise, in a final *coup de théâtre*, the priest is informed that his master, Zeus Sōtēr himself, has had the same idea and is already on earth,[106] presumably looking for food.

Many ideas of salvation seem to have been of democratic origin.[107] This can be seen, for instance, in the proposals of Euaion and Blepyros, the essence of which is taking from the rich and giving to the poor.[108] This is perfectly in line with the spirit of the radical Athenian democracy.

---

[101] *Eccl.* 396; 401-2; 412-14; cf. 202; 219.

[102] *Plut.* 463; cf. 878-9. For Panhellenic elements in Aristophanic comedy, see W. M. Hugill, *Panhellenism in Aristophanes* (diss. Chicago, 1936). For the universal purpose of conferring a blessing on all mankind by restoring Wealth's sight, see *Plut.* 461; 464; cf. 144-6; 490; see also Th. Gelzer, *RE* Suppl. XII (1970), s.v. "Aristophanes", col. 1505. On Athens' still being Aristophanes' focus of interest with respect to the salvation theme, see, e.g., *Plut.* 627; 771ff.; 1192.

[103] *Eccl.* 79; 761; 1045; 1103; *Plut.* 877; 1175; 1186; 1189.

[104] See above, n. 57.

[105] *Plut.* 327: "σωτῆρες τοῦ θεοῦ".

[106] *Plut.* 1175ff.; 1189f.

[107] This was suggested (without discussion) by P. Cloché, "La démocratie athénienne et les possédants aux Vᵉ et IVᵉ siècles avant J.C.", *RH* 192 (1941), p. 25f.; C. Mossé, *La fin de la démocratie athénienne* (Paris, 1962), p. 240f., rejects the idea "... parce que le 'communisme' du IVᵉ siècle n'a rien d'une doctrine démocratique, mais apparaît au contraire chez des penseurs aristocratiques". However, this argument does not seem convincing; see the discussion below.

[108] For the description of democracy as the rule of the poor over the rich and over their possessions, see, e.g., Ps.-Xen. *Ath. Pol.* 1, 2-5; 13-14; 2, 9-10; 18-19; 3, 10-11; Plat. *Resp.* 557A, 565A; 565E-566A; Arist. *Pol.* 1279b 8ff.; 1320a 5ff.; 17ff.; cf. Newman, *The Politics of Aristotle*, IV, p. 530f.

Euaion's proposals are explicitly described as "most democratic".[109] To a considerable extent Praxagora's programme may be regarded as a *reductio ad absurdum* of such proposals, and the heroine herself describes her innovations as democratic.[110] Moreover, later on in the play, after the foundation of the new regime, it is clearly referred to as a democracy.[111]

Within the context of his discussion of democracies in the *Politics*, Aristotle provides evidence for the practice of the rich sharing their property with the poor. However, this practice is to be found not only in democracies but also in non-democratic states, as is evident from the examples enlisted by Aristotle himself.[112] It should be noted that the theory advocating the sharing of property by the rich with the poor was adopted by Greek intellectuals (such as Plato, Isokrates and Aristotle) whose attitude towards democracy, especially radical democracy, can hardly be described as enthusiastic.[113]

Moreover, some of the "communist" ideas in Athens may well have been of aristocratic origin. During the fifth century the idealization of Sparta had already been adopted by aristocratic circles as an ideological weapon against Athenian democracy. The eulogy of Spartan political and social institutions, way of life, education and norms of behaviour—all of which included certain egalitarian or collectivist patterns—was for many Athenian aristocrats a sort of salon-Laconism, which was motivated by their opposition to democracy rather than by genuine love of Sparta.[114] This did not mean that the Spartan legend

---

[109] *Eccl.* 411: "ἔλεξε δημοτικωτάτους λόγους".

[110] *Eccl.* 631: "δημοτικὴ γ' ἡ γνώμη". This characterization applies to sexual "communism", but there is no reason to limit the implication only to this area; after all, sexual "communism" is an integral part of the whole equalitarian system. See next note.

[111] *Eccl.* 945: "δημοκρατούμεθα".

[112] *Pol.* 1320 a17-b17. The examples given by Aristotle within this context are those of the Carthaginians and of the Tarentines. The latter are said to make their property "communal for the purpose of use by the poor". Other examples for common use of property are those of the Spartans and of the Cretans (*ibid.* 1263a 35ff.; b40ff.; cf. Newman, *The Politics of Aristotle* II, p. 248; A. Fuks, "The Sharing of Property by the Rich with the Poor in Greek Theory and Practice", *SCI* 5 (1979/80), p. 55ff.

[113] See, e.g., Plat. *Leg.* 736D; Isocr. *Areop.* 31-35; 54-55; Arist. *Pol.* 1320b 2-3; cf. 1263a 22; 1320a 11ff., and see Fuks, *ibid.* p. 46f.; 51ff., with further evidence and bibliography.

[114] They could hardly have lived according to the rules of the Spartan diet. Kritias is the most prominent exponent of these circles, and the loss of his writings, with the exception of a few passages which have survived through later quotations, makes it difficult for us to reconstruct the precise patterns of the Spartan legend as fostered by late fifth-century upper-class ideology, including its views on the collectivist and equalitarian features of Sparta. If we are to form an opinion on the basis of the evidence provided by the slightly later writings of Xenophon—who may partially be regarded as another representative of Athenian upper-class attitudes—the above traits of Sparta had most probably also been praised by his predecessors. The same is true—*mutatis mutandis*—with respect to Plato (see

could not be used eventually—now that the times had changed following the complete failure of two oligarchic revolutions—for other purposes, which were not incompatible with the spirit of the Athenian democracy.

The basic idea of citizens-peers (homoioi),[115] the common messes (syssitia),[116] certain customs and norms concerning common use of property[117] or sharing of wives and children[118]—all these could inspire and did actually inspire, in many cases, the development of "communist" ideas outside Sparta. It is well known that the imitation of these patterns often went far beyond the original Spartan model.[119]

The imitation of Sparta is not a new motif in Aristophanes. In earlier plays he had ridiculed the lakōnomania of superficially imitating Spartan customs, especially those connected with personal appearance, clothes, diet and style.[120] Spartan fashion is also mentioned several times in the Ekklesiazousai. Praxagora seems to be obsessed particularly, and typically, with Laconian red shoes.[121] But it is not only Spartan fashion she seems to be interested in. The basic idea of living the same, common and equal way of life is closely connected with the Spartan concept of diaita and of homoioi,[122] although nothing could be further removed from the austerity of the Spartan diet than the hedonistic content of the life-style envisaged by Praxagora. The idea of exempting the citizens from productive work, which is left only for the slaves, is also reminiscent of Sparta, but the purpose of acquiring leisure from work is completely different: it is not to enable the citizen to devote his life to military service and political activity, but to indulge in a parasitic life-style.

The theme of the Ekklesiazousai provided Aristophanes with an exceptional occasion for presenting, among other things, a caricature of the most typically collectivist of Sparta's institutions—the syssitia—as losing its basic characteristic of austerity when adapted to Athenian

---

below). For the fragments of Kritias' works, see Diels-Kranz, II[6], p. 371-99; 426-28; On Kritias and Sparta, see esp. F. Ollier, Le mirage spartiate I (Paris, 1933), p. 169ff.; E. N. Tigerstedt, The Legend of Sparta in Classical Antiquity (Stockholm, 1965), p. 165ff.; 435f.

[115] On equality in Sparta and its limits, see David, Sparta between Empire and Revolution, p. 44ff., with bibliography.

[116] On the Spartan syssitia, see id., "The Spartan Syssitia and Plato's Laws", AJP 99 (1978), p. 486ff., with bibliography.

[117] See Xen. Lac. Pol. 6, 3-4; Arist. loc. cit. (above, n. 112).

[118] See Xen. Lac. Pol. 1, 6-9; Polyb. 12, 6b, 8; Plut. Lyc. 15.

[119] As, for instance, in the case of Plato's Republic; see David, Sparta between Empire and Revolution, p. 64f.

[120] Vesp. 474-76, 1157ff.; Av. 1280ff.; cf. Plat. Prot. 342B-C; cf. Ollier, Le mirage spartiate, p. 182ff.; Tigerstedt, The Legend of Sparta I, p. 123f.

[121] Eccl. 74; 269; 345-6; 405; 508; 542; cf. Ussher, Eccl. p. 85; Sartori, "Elementi storici" (above, n. 1), p. 335.

[122] See, e.g., Eccl. 594: "ἀλλ' ἕνα ποιῶ κοινὸν πᾶσιν βίοτον καὶ τοῦτον ὅμοιον"; cf. Lévy, Athènes devant la défaite, p. 208, n. 2.

hedonism.[123] The same is true—*mutatis mutandis*—with respect to the Spartan norms of behaviour concerning sexual life: the possibility of sharing wives, husbands and children. But the Spartan examples of "sexual communism" are isolated and pale[124] in comparison with Praxagora's claim to abolish the institution of the family altogether. Her absolute sexual communism for all citizens has not only taken up certain Spartan features, carrying them to extremes, but has also stripped them of their original meaning and given them a new aim—the equal gratification of sexual desire.

Aristophanes intended to show his audience, among other things, a caricature resulting from the imitation of certain traditional features of Sparta, which previously had been praised only by narrow aristocratic circles in Athens. Now certain Spartan patterns were probably held up as an example by those who preached egalitarian and collectivist solutions as a way to *sōtēria*. The growing popularity of such propaganda may be explained by the affinities between some of its basic ideas and some levelling elements in the spirit of Athenian democracy.

To sum up—the ideas parodied by Aristophanes in the *Ekklesiazousai* do not belong to a philosophical treatise. They seem to be a complex mixture, an amalgam of contemporary schemes and proposals stemming from various sources of inspiration, but having a common aim: to find a way to salvation from the difficult crisis in which Athens found itself at the time. Aristophanes' audience was familiar with the ideas parodied on the stage; consequently the playwright was exempt from specifying the target, or targets, of his satire.

We have tried to show the weakness of the view that the *Ekklesiazousai* was a parody of Plato's "communistic" ideas. This does not imply that we are ignoring a possible, even probable, link between Plato and Aristophanes, but this link has to be interpreted with due respect to chronology. It is obvious that Plato's object in the *Republic* was far more

---

[123] *Eccl.* 676; 715; 834ff.; 1167ff.; cf. Ussher, *Eccl.* p. 170f. Plato adopted the institution of *syssitia* both in the state of the *Republic* and in that of the *Laws*, but his *syssitia* are highly different from those founded by Praxagora. His aims in adopting the *syssitia* were to achieve a high degree of uniformity and moderation, to enforce the principle of equality (or relative equality) and the elements of public order and discipline. His *syssitia* are certainly inspired by those of the so-called "Lycurgan" Sparta. See David, "The Spartan *Syssitia* ..." (above, n. 116), p. 487f.

[124] See above, n. 110. To be sure, Sparta did not provide the only examples of sexual "communism" known to the Greeks. Herodotus (4, 104) mentions that "the Agathyrsians have their women in common, so that they may be brothers to one another, and being all kinsmen, show no envy or hatred to one another". Moreover, in a fragment of Euripides' *Protesilaos*, one of the characters advocated the view that women should be common to all men: see A. Nauck, *Tragicorum Graecorum Fragmenta²*, fr. 563. See also Newman, *The Politics of Aristotle*, II, p. 282.

profound than simply to react to the play, but this does not allow us to dismiss the strong probability that he had taken the comedy into consideration when writing his masterpiece.[125]

There are some passages in the fifth book of the *Republic* which have been wrongly interpreted as a violent invective on the part of Plato against Aristophanes.[126] The philosopher mentions the possibility of ridiculing the idea of women exercising naked in the palaestra along with the men, and adds; "We must not be afraid of all the jokes with which the wits might greet so great a change"; and again: "The man who ridicules naked women practicing gymnastics ... plucks the unripe fruit of laughter."[127] In another passage the idea is expressed, once more in the context of gymnastics, but in more general terms: "... he is empty who believes anything ridiculous other than the bad, and who tries to raise laughter by regarding any sight ridiculous which is neither foolish nor bad."[128]

There is no proof whatsoever in any of these passages or elsewhere that the philosopher's invective was directed against Aristophanes. The context of these references (i.e., women's athletic exercises) can only testify against this interpretation, for such a subject was at no time ridiculed in the *Ekklesiazousai*. Moreover, the above references cannot logically be considered a counter-attack of Plato on Aristophanes, because a counter-attack presupposes an attack and, as we have seen, the playwright had not ridiculed the philosopher.

The passages quoted above seem to suggest that Plato is defending himself, not against Aristophanes, but against a possible and unjustified imitation or abuse of comic methods to ridicule his own ideas. The philosopher is said to have held Aristophanes in high esteem.[129]

[125] See esp. Adam, *Republic*, p. 349ff. and Koster, *op. cit.* (above, n. 93), p. 22ff., with whom my views happen to coincide on certain points although they differ as to the conclusion. See below.

[126] See Adam, *ibid.* p. 349, following Chiapelli (*loc. cit.*, above, n. 93): "it is difficult to resist the impression that Plato's vigorous invective, though professedly general, has also a personal implication". Adam is referring to the passages quoted below; see nn. 127-8.

[127] *Resp.* 452 B-C; 457B.

[128] *Resp.* 452D.

[129] Despite the treatment of his beloved master in the *Clouds*, which he had not forgotten (see Plat. *Apol.* 18B; 19C). He was aware that the danger of abuse is a general problem of Aristophanes' *genre* and not his personal vice (see *ibid.* and also *locc. citt.* in nn. 127, 128). Later, in the *Symposium*, Plato depicted a sympathetic picture of Aristophanes. The philosopher's admiration for the comic poet is also attested—for what it is worth—by biographical tradition. See D. L. Page, *Epigrammata Graeca* (Oxford, 1975), p. 51, Plato, XIV (= 14 Diehl) for the epigram attributed to Plato, which says that the Graces, having looked for a temple that would never fall, found the soul of Aristophanes: "Αἱ Χάριτες, τέμενός τι λαβεῖν ὅπερ οὐχὶ πεσεῖται ζητοῦσαι, ψυχὴν ηὗρον Ἀριστοφάνους." Plato is said to have recommended Aristophanes' comedies to Dionysios, the tyrant of Syracuse, as the best source for a study of Athens. See *Vita* 25 (F. Dübner, *Scholia Graeca in Aristophanem*

Moreover, he would have been the first to agree with the playwright's criticism of Praxagora's type of "communism".

However, despite the essential dissimilarity between Plato's type of "communism" and that envisaged by Praxagora, the philosopher could find some of the arguments advanced by her in defence of her own "communism" as applicable also to the defence of his proposals, in the *Republic*, and even as worthy of being put there into Sokrates' mouth.[129a]

5. *Misthos Ekklesiastikos*

It is obvious from what has already been said that Aristophanes' last extant plays are social comedies *par excellence*. The playwright's focus of interest is on politics no longer. And even when a central political motif, such as the *misthos ekklesiastikos* is raised, the treatment is largely, even mainly, from the social point of view.

The *misthophoria* is not a new motif in Aristophanes' last comedies. This characteristic trait of radical democracy was the object of satire and criticism in some of his earlier plays, especially in the *Wasps*, where the *misthos dikastikos*, the payment of the jurors, is frequently mentioned.[130] A hostile attitude towards *misthophoria* was characteristic not only of the extreme oligarchs during the Peloponnesian War, but also of the moderate opponents to Athenian democracy.[131] Like the latter, Aristophanes seems to have believed that despite its faults and vices, democracy was not irremediable.[132] Later, during the fourth century, an averse attitude

---

(Paris, 1842), Prol. p. XII. If the story is true, Plato seems to have been the first to appreciate the great value of Aristophanic comedy as an historical source. For the resemblance of certain views of Plato to those of the playwright, see also nn. 70; 133; 149; 200; 206.

[129a] See above, and n. 55.

[130] See, e.g., *Eq.* 50-1; 255-7; 797-800; 805-8; 1358-60; *Nub.* 863; *Vesp.* 300-11; 525; 606-9; 661-3; 682-4; 689-90; 784-5; 813; 1117-21; *Av.* 1541.

[131] See, e.g., Ps.-Xen. *Ath. Pol.* 1, 3; Thuc. 8. 67, 3; 97, 1-2; Arist. *Ath. Pol.* 29, 5; 33; cf. Xen. *Hell.* 2, 3, 48.

[132] In the *Knights*, for instance, which contains his sharpest attack on radical democracy and its leaders, the demagogues, he nevertheless expressed at the end of the play his belief in the possibility of reforming the existing regime (witness the *volte-face* of the Sausage-Seller and of old Demos). Moreover, he never called for the overthrow of democracy, even on the eve of the first oligarchic revolution, when he had nothing to fear (witness the balanced and moderate political position in *Lysistrata*, which was produced in 411 B.C. ll.571ff.). There is no basis for the thesis which attempted to present the playwright as a staunch supporter of the oligarchs; see, e.g., Couat, *Aristophane*, p. 46ff. and *passim*; but see the criticism of, e.g., Croiset, *Aristophanes*, p. 15ff. and n. 1; cf. Ste. Croix, *The Origins of the Peloponnesian War*, p. 357ff.; see also below, nn. 187, 189, for Aristophanes' admiration of Thrasyboulos, the politician who played the decisive role in the liberation of Athens from the rule of the "Thirty Tyrants" and in the restoration of the democratic regime.

towards the *misthophoria* was inherited by various critics of the Athenian democracy.[133]

The criticism of *misthophoria* is yet another example of an old motif which is given new dimensions in Aristophanes' last plays. The new treatment was occasioned by a political innovation of the late fifth or early fourth century, shortly after the end of the Peloponnesian War: the introduction of a motion by a demagogue, Agyrrhios, to pay a fee to the citizens for their attendance at the assemblies. The fee was, at first, one obol; later it was raised by the political initiative of another politician, Herakleides, to two obols, and, finally, Agyrrhios sponsored the measure that the *misthos ekklesiastikos* be raised to three obols.[134] Consequently, he strengthened, for the time being, his political influence. Aristophanes' antipathy for Agyrrhios[135] may be explained by his almost instinctive, even pathological dislike of contemporary demagogues.[136] The *misthos ekklesiastikos* is presented several times in Aristophanes' last extant plays, especially in the *Ekklesiazousai*, as a symptom of the growing individualism and egocentric materialism of the citizens, as well as the encouragement of these phenomena by demagogues. Despite his aspiration to win the first prize in the dramatic competition, Aristophanes had the courage, now as in the past, to say hard things to his audience, such as, for instance: "Now that you are paid out of public funds each of you seeks only his private gain";[137] "Is not the Assembly held through him?" (viz. Wealth); "Does not Agyrrhios flout us all for him?"[138] "We are disposed rather to take than to give, just like the gods; look at their statues stretching out their hands".[139]

---

[133] See, e.g., Plat. *Gorg.* 515E; Isocr. *Areop.* 24-25; Arist. *Pol.* 1300 a 2-3; 1317b 30ff.; *Ath. Pol.* 27, 3-5.

[134] Arist. *Ath. Pol.* 41, 3; Aristoph. *Eccl.* 183-5; 302; Agyrrhios' career was reconstructed by W. H. Hess, *Studies in the Ecclesiazusae of Aristophanes* (diss. Princeton, 1962), a work which has not been accessible to me except in its abstract (*Diss. Abstr.* 25 (1964), p. 460, cf. Ussher, *Eccl.* p. 101). See now also P. J. Rhodes, *A Commentary on the Aristotelian Athenaion Politeia* (Oxford, 1981), p. 492.

[135] See *Eccl.* 102; 175-6; 184-5; *Plut.* 176. Ussher, *ibid.*, rejects the attempt of W. H. Hess to present Agyrrhios as "the focal point of the political satire" in *Eccl.* as very unconvincing. Agyrrhios, far from being a real substitute for Kleon, is only a secondary target in the play.

[136] It has been argued that Aristophanes' attitude towards him may also have been influenced by his role in lowering the comic poets' payment; see *Ra.* 367, with scholiast; Pl. Com. fr. 133 (Kock); cf. Couat, *Aristophane*, p. 51; Ussher, *loc. cit.* (above, n. 134). However, none of Aristophanes' explicit attacks on him makes mention of this issue.

[137] *Eccl.* 205-7; cf. ll. 303-10, where the present is contrasted with the good old days of Athens, when the citizens, though far from being rich, were eager to attend the meetings of the Assembly and serve the State, without being paid for this.

[138] *Plut.* 171; 176.

[139] *Eccl.* 778-80. Within its dramatic context, this remark is one of the arguments advanced by the anonymous citizen in order to convince Chremes that most of the Athe-

Paying the citizens for coming to the Assembly can be seen not only as a demagogic means of gaining popularity and political influence, but also as an attempt to find a solution to the problem of political apathy, and help fill the Assemblies: "There was a time we did not bother to come to the Assemblies at all but then, at least, we knew Agyrrhios was a rogue".[140] Only when the fee was raised by Agyrrhios to three obols did it become effective, and the meetings of the Assembly again became crowded.[141] Political apathy could partly have been a consequence of the mental atmosphere after Athens' defeat in the Peloponnesian War. However, this phenomenon could also have been caused and certainly encouraged by the economic crisis. Aristophanes did not ignore the connection. between the *misthos ekklesiastikos* and the economic situation: Blepyros, for instance, accuses his wife of having deprived him of the portion of wheat he could have bought with his fee had he been able to go to the Assembly;[142] those citizens who fail to arrive at the Pnyx by break of day will forfeit their fee and will have to carry home their shopping baskets empty.[143] The problem is not new: Philokleon, the old juryman in the *Wasps*, tried to avoid this calamity by sleeping all night in front of the court.[144] However, the dimensions of the problem have changed: it is no longer the case of some old jurymen only, but of a large section within the citizen-body. As we have seen, Aristophanes was well aware of the existence of poverty and of its severe symptoms. However, paying the masses for coming to the Assembly does not seem to him the proper way to solve the problem of political apathy. This kind of solution is presented as dangerous, not only because it helps certain demagogues gain a reputation and political influence unjustly deserved, but also, and perhaps mainly, because it encourages the greed of the masses. Hence the measure defeats its own purpose: instead of working against the individualistic tendencies and the political apathy of the time, it ultimately helps to encourage them.

The *misthos ekklesiastikos*, although frequently mentioned in the *Ekklesiazousai*, is far from being the main theme of the play.[145] It is,

---

nians will not give up their private property. However, the remark is not an isolated one, representing only the viewpoint of this citizen, but is consonant with the general spirit of the playwright's criticism of contemporary Athenian society in his last plays.

[140] *Eccl.* 183-5.

[141] *Eccl.* 185-8; 300-10, *Plut.* 171, 329-30.

[142] *Eccl.* 547-8.

[143] *Eccl.* 289ff.; cf. 379ff.

[144] *Vesp.* 103-5.

[145] W. H. Hess, *loc. cit.* (above, n. 134), believes that the introduction of the ecclesiastic pay occasioned the play, which is hardly acceptable. This view seems to be logically connected with his opinion on Agyrrhios' role in the play (see above, n. 135).

however, closely connected, both in the *Ekklesiazousai* and in the *Ploutos*, with central themes, since it helps the playwright to stress the prevalent condition of poverty and the mentality of egocentric materialism in contemporary Athenian society.

In the *Ekklesiazousai*, these central themes are similarly emphasized in the proposals put forward by Euaion and Blepyros and, especially, in Praxagora's programme.

6. *The Censure of Materialism*

It has been argued in the literature that Praxagora's programme is not to be taken as a "glutton's Paradise", and that her offer is "a remedy, not a complete switch from poverty to wealth".[146] This view appears to be based on a confusion between Aristophanes' opinions and those of his heroine. What she promises, and, especially, the way her programme is implemented, goes far beyond merely satisfying the basic necessities of life. In fact we are faced with an outburst of unbridled materialism, which is refuted by Aristophanes in the very way he presents it: the ludicrous transformation of the political function of the city's public places into a gastronomical function;[147] the obsession with the idea of the copious banquet, and the details of the rich menu served at the luxurious *syssitia*;[148] all these, and the general idea of reducing human activities to food and sex, make the impression that the so-called "glutton's Paradise" is considered by Aristophanes as a bestial Hell of gourmand and libidinous parasites. Within this context it is worth stressing once more that Plato would have agreed with Aristophanes' criticism of this sort of "communism". Indulgent hedonism was wholly foreign to Plato's mind, as can be seen in all of his works.[149]

In the *Ploutos*, the presentation of the materialistic mentality prevalent in contemporary Athens is even more manifest. Everyone and everything is believed by Chremylos and Karion—both of whom reflect a wide-

---

[146] See, e.g., Ehrenberg, *The People of Aristophanes*, p. 70: "... modest bourgeois enjoyments" and esp. Ussher, *Eccl.* p. 160; cf. M. M. Mactoux, *Douleia* (Paris, 1980), p. 153.

[147] *Eccl.* 676ff.

[148] *Eccl.* 834ff.; 1116ff.; 1136ff.; and especially 1167ff., where one of the dishes has a name seven lines long.

[149] From this viewpoint it is worth paying special attention to Plato's comments on his first visit to Syracuse, where, by the way, he is said to have recommended the reading of Aristophanes (see above, n. 129); he was shocked by the sort of life considered there as happy, especially by the excesses in food and sex. He stresses his disapproval of a city whose citizens find it appropriate to spend everything on excesses, avoiding all industry with the exception of that devoted to banquets and to the gratification of sexual desires (*Epist. VII*, 326 B-D).

spread attitude—to depend solely upon Wealth. Zeus rules over the gods only by virtue of his silver; men sacrifice to him only for the sake of wealth; no man ever has enough of wealth. Everything in the world that is bright and fair owes its existence to Wealth,[150] the god who, by the way, is paradoxically presented as extremely ugly and dirty.[151] The audience is actually faced with the portrait of a beggar ironically intended to incarnate Wealth.

The blind god is also presented as extremely weak, even as a coward, but again, paradoxically, it is to him that every mortal thing is subject.[152] Even the Great King owes his power to him, and wars are won by that whom Wealth favours.[153]

These remarks deserve special attention as important examples of Aristophanes' ability to combine recent political and international topics with socio-economic themes. The comments are certainly based on the crucial role that Persian money played in the recent past in Greece. The victory of Sparta in the Peloponnesian War would have been impossible without Persian subsidies.[154] Persians money was also an important factor on the eve of the Corinthian War, when Persia, now at war with her former ally, was interested in bringing about the formation of a large anti-Spartan league in Greece, and sent, for this purpose, an agent whose mission was to bribe influential politicians in several Greek cities.[155] Also, during the Corinthian War, Persian money was a major factor in support of the anti-Spartan alliance, especially since it helped Athens to rebuild the Long Walls and fortify the Piraeus.[156] The *Ploutos* was composed shortly before the "King's Peace", but the Spartans had already realized the capital importance of Persian support for the renewal of their hegemony and had started directing their efforts towards a new *entente* with Persia.[157] The financial situation of Athens and her ability to wage

---

[150] *Plut.* 130-1; 134-43; 193; 144-61.

[151] *Plut.* 80; 83-5.

[152] *Plut.* 122ff.; 146; cf. U. Albini, "La struttura del *Pluto* di Aristofane", *PP* 20 (1965), p. 432: "... un doppio effetto drammatico: da un lato lo spettatore sa che il dio introdotto sulla scena non è un dio, ma il più forte degli dèi; dall'altro sa che è debole, perché cieco e inconsapevole del suo potere".

[153] *Plut.* 170; 184.

[154] On the Persian subsidies to Sparta during the last years of the Peloponnesian War, see E. David, "The Influx of Money into Sparta at the End of the Fifth Century B.C.", *SCI* 5 (1979/80), p. 31ff., with evidence.

[155] Xen. *Hell.* 3, 5, 1-2, 4, 2, 1, *Hell. Oxy.* 2, 2, 2, 5, cf. 13, 1; Plut. *Lys.* 27, 1; Polyaen. 1, 78; cf. S. Perlman, "The Causes and Outbreak of the Corinthian War", *CQ* 14 (1964), p. 64ff.; C. D. Hamilton, *Sparta's Bitter Victories. Politics and Diplomacy in the Corinthian War* (Ithaca, N.Y., 1979), p. 179ff.; 198f.

[156] Xen. *Hell.* 4, 8, 9-12.

[157] *Ibid.* 12-16; cf. T. T. B. Ryder, *Koine Eirene* (Oxford, 1965), p. 27-31; App. XII, p. 165ff.; Hamilton, *op. cit.* p. 233ff.; 301ff.

the war had seriously deteriorated at the end of the nineties, when Persia stopped sending the subsidies. To cope with the new situation, a tax of 1/40th was imposed in order to raise 500 talents. The imposition of this tax (probably an indirect one) is an important piece of evidence provided by Aristophanes. He ascribes the fiscal initiative to a certain Euripides (active in the 390s), who is said to have been popular for a time, until this tax proved to be insufficient for raising the above sum.[158] Subsequently, it was decided to collect a direct war-tax.[159]

Aristophanes puts into the mouth of his heroes additional comments on the power of Wealth, which are obviously inspired by recent social and political developments in Athens and in other parts of Greece. It is stated, as we have seen, that the Assembly owes its quorum to Wealth.[160] And besides, "Does he not feed the foreign troops at Corinth?"[161] This is a clear allusion to the mercenary force which had been raised by Konon and installed at Corinth in 393 B.C. These mercenaries had recently succeeded, under the command of Iphikrates, in inflicting a crushing defeat upon a regiment of Spartan hoplites.[162]

The growing use of mercenary soldiers instead of citizens is, on the one hand, an additional symptom of poverty, since many Greeks in search of

---

[158] *Eccl.* 823-9; for the probability that an indirect taxation is meant, see R. Thomsen, *Eisphora. A Study of Direct Taxation in Ancient Athens* (Copenhagen, 1964), p. 184, with further literature. Within the same context, Aristophanes mentions two other abortive resolutions, about which very little is known. The first resolution, whose precise date is impossible to establish on a firm basis, was concerned with salt (*Eccl.* 814); according to the scholiast (*ad loc.*), this was intended to control the price of salt and keep it low, but was ineffective. The second resolution dealt with the issuing of copper coins, and its date is highly problematic. The suggestion to connect these copper coins with the effects of the capture of Dekeleia by the Spartans and the subsequent inability of the Athenians to get at their silver mines in Laureion (see *Ra.* 720; 725; Ussher, *Eccl.* p. 188, with further literature) encounters, *pace* Ussher, the difficulty of being too distant to be mentioned in *Eccl.* There is also no evidence for Ehrenberg's dating of the decree withdrawing the copper coinage (i.e., proclaiming the return to silver)—*Eccl.* 822—in 393 B.C. (*The People of Aristophanes*, p. 222 and Plate XVIIIC). This date is strange in view of the fact that Ehrenberg accepts the above date of the resolution concerning those copper coins (i.e., connects it with *Ra.* 720; 5), whereas Aristophanes makes it quite clear that this resolution was in vigour only a short time. What can be said for certain is that both the salt resolution and those connected with coinage were passed before the tax resolution (*Eccl.* 823) and that all of the resolutions mentioned in this part of the play were shortlived. Only for curiosity's sake—Urbain, "Les idées économiques d'Aristophane" (above, n. 23), sees the above passage dealing with the coinage as sufficient evidence for crediting the playwright with the precocious knowledge of "Gresham's Law" (cf. Nicosia, *Economia e Politica*, p. 199. On Euripides, cf. Davies, *Athenian Propertied Families*, p. 202.

[159] Isocr. *Trap.* 41; cf. H. Francotte, *Les finances des cités grecques* (Paris, 1909), p. 28, n. 1.

[160] *Plut.* 171; see also above, n. 141.

[161] *Plut.* 173.

[162] Xen. *Hell.* 4, 5, 3-17; 8, 7; cf. Rogers, *Plut.* p. 20.

a livelihood were compelled to choose this profession.[163] On the other hand, it is also a symptom of the decline of patriotism, and of the growth of individualistic materialism. The most extreme expression of this trend is to be found in the personality of Hermes.[164] When asked if he really approves of deserting to the enemy, he gives the prompt answer, "Every land where a man prospers is his native land."[165]

Aristophanes believed that the roots of this crude materialism were to be found both in extreme wealth and in abject poverty. The wealthy were indifferent to the interests of the state; many of them were even ready to act against the interests of the community.[166] In the speech Against Philon, delivered shortly after the restoration of democracy (in 403 B.C.), Lysias had already referred to those who "adopt the view that any country in which they have their business is their homeland; these are evidently men who would abandon the public interest (to koinon agathon) of their city to seek their private gain because they regard their property, not their city, as their homeland."[167]

The poor, on the other hand, were brutalized by the miserable conditions under which they lived and could only think of what they needed most—food. This is also illustrated in a passage from an unknown play of Aristophanes which belongs, most probably, to the same period (i.e., early fourth century): "Whichever homeland gives food to the poor, saving him from hunger, is dear to him."[168]

Not only patriotism was jeopardized and undermined by the new mentality of individualistic materialism—engendered both by excessive wealth and by degrading poverty; basic human values such as familial affection, love and friendship were also endangered. Money had become much more important than mutual assistance between relatives and friends.[169] The leading character in the Ploutos, Chremylos, is made to confess that he adores wealth more than his wife and only son.[170]

---

[163] See, e.g., Isocr. Paneg. 168; cf. ibid. 115-6; see also id. Archid. 76; Pax, 24; 46-48 Phil. 96; cf. Fuks, "Isokrates and Greece" (above, n. 83), p. 26ff., with further evidence.

[164] Plut. 1118-9.

[165] Plut. 1151: "πατρὶς γάρ ἐστι πᾶσ'ἵν' ἂν πράττῃ τις εὖ". (cf. the more famous Roman dictum, containing the same idea, ap. Cic. Tusc. 5, 37, 108: "patria est ubicumque est bene").

[166] Plut. 569-70, and see above nn. 70-5; cf. Plat. Resp. 421E-422A.

[167] Lys. 31 (in Phil.), 6: "διὰ τὸ μὴ τὴν πόλιν ἀλλὰ τὴν οὐσίαν πατρίδα ἑαυτοῖς ἡγεῖσθαι".

[168] J. Demiańczuk, Supplementum Comicum (Cracow, 1912), Aristoph. fr. 58 (= Stob. 2, 10, 2a): "πατρὶς δὲ πᾶσα τῷ πένητι προσφιλής ἀφ'ἧς τροφήν τε καὶ τὸ μὴ πεινῆν ἔχει". Cf. Metagenes ap. Athen. 6, 271A = Kock, I, fr. 18: "one omen is best, to fight for one's dinner" (cf. Lévy, op. cit. p. 224f.). For the base attitude of mind and moral degeneration as caused by extreme poverty, see also Plat. Resp. 422A; 465 B-C; cf. Fuks, "The Conditions of Riches and of Poverty" (above, n. 86), p. 70f. See also Isocr. Antid. 142 ("Some men have been so brutalized by envy and want ..."); cf. ibid. 24.

[169] Plut. 239-41; 834-6.

[170] Plut. 250-1.

Aristophanes addresses his audience through the mouth of one of his characters, speaking more like a prophet than a comedian: "Alas! how utterly wanting in honesty everyone is. The love of money overcomes us all."[171]

Even the gods are anthropomorphically depicted in the *Ploutos* as immoral, egocentric and materialist, their mentality being a copy of that prevalent in contemporary Athenian society. Hermes is not the only example. The portrait of his master, Zeus, is no less impressive from this viewpoint. And, as we have seen, the playwright explicitly compared the mentality of men to that of the gods, whose statues, stretching out their hands, reveal their readiness to take rather than to give.[172]

Some scholars have advanced the erroneous view that Aristophanes himself was a representative of individualistic materialism, and of its victory over political ideals.[173] However, as we have seen, the playwright regarded individualistic materialism as a plague. The materialist solution of Praxagora's "communism" is severely censured, not only because of its impracticability, but also, and mainly, because of its very essence.

There is, it is true, a scene in the *Ploutos*—that in which the sycophant is presented in confrontation with the Honest Man (Dikaios Anēr)—which can mislead, and has caused several scholars to conclude that the author was in favour of an apolitical ideal,[174] like that recommended to the hyperactivist sycophant: to live in peace and quiet, not to meddle in other people's affairs.[175] Nevertheless, Aristophanes' attack on the sycophant's *polypragmosynē* does not imply a general attack on political activism, or a belief that honest citizens should stick only to their private business. Witness, for instance, his deep sympathy for the citizens of

---

[171] *Plut.* 362-3. To be sure, when taken within its dramatic context, this remark contains an element of dramatic irony, since the speaker, Blepsidemos, unjustly suspects his friend, Chremylos, of being dishonest, and the audience knows that in this case the suspicion is unfounded. However, over and above this specific function, Blepsidemos' remark is a vehicle for conveying a general view of the playwright, which is after all expressed in many other passages of the play, through the mouth of various *dramatis personae*.

[172] See above, nn. 57; 139. On Aristophanes' attitude towards the gods, see also K. McLeish, *The Theatre of Aristophanes* (London, 1980), p. 58f.

[173] See esp. Ehrenberg, *The People of Aristophanes*, p. 323: "A. in his old age praised Wealth as the great giver of prosperity and happiness, and approved of, even glorified, the desire for wealth ..."; cf. p. 319: "A. apparently fights for an unpolitical ideal ..."; cf. p. 350: "A. was fundamentally a representative of an individualistic materialism akin to the creed he attacked in the teachings of the sophists"; cf. *id.* "Polypragmosyne: A Study in Greek Politics", *JHS* 67 (1947), p. 54f.; Cataudella, "Due note ad Aristofane" (above, n. 76), p. 203; R. Cantarella, "L'ultimo Aristofane", *Dioniso* 40 (1966), p. 41; Lévy, *Athènes devant la défaite*, p. 232ff.: "Dans le *Ploutos* la politique est déjà assimilée à la *polypragmosyne*"; cf. p. 256.

[174] *locc. citt.* in the previous note.

[175] *Plut.* 921; cf. 910.

good old days, who were eager to play their part in public affairs and serve the state without being paid for this.[175a]

The sycophant is censured precisely because, by the very definition of his "profession", he abuses political activism for his own individual profit. Dramatically he is confronted with the figure of the Honest Man. The latter had tried to be useful to society by helping his friends with money and, consequently, became a pauper.[176] The sycophant argues that he is useful to society because he superintends the law[177] but, in fact, this sort of "usefulness" consisted of making money by blackmail, and growing rich at the expense of his fellow-citizens. The very moment he appears on the stage he complains he is ruined because Wealth has regained his sight:[178] now he can no longer enrich himself by his denunciations and his prosecutions. He has learnt no trade at all; the only way he can earn a living is "to be in charge of all private and public matters."[179] The sycophant presents himself as a patriot (*philopolis*),[180] but this kind of patriotism is false. He claims he would not give up his activity even for Wealth in person,[181] but the very motivation of sycophancy is lust for wealth, which, in this case, is coupled with an incurable mania for prosecution and for *polypragmosynē*.

The presentation of the sycophant is a caricature of a political ideal which has been abused and distorted; the target of Aristophanes' satire

---

[175a] *Eccl.* 303-10.

[176] *Plut.* 827-33. This danger of *euergesia* was probably a subject of discussion at the time; cf. Anon. Iamb. in Diels-Kranz, II⁶, 89, 4-6; see also Cataudella, *op. cit.* p. 201 and Lévy, *op. cit.* p. 249.

[177] *Plut.* 900; 907-15; cf. Anon. Iamb., *ibid.*, who asks the question how can a man be useful without distributing money and answers that real usefulness is to be found in the guardianship of the laws and of justice. See also Cataudella, *ibid.* p. 200ff., who stresses the similarity between certain concepts and confrontations in the above text and in the *Ploutos* (see also above, n. 76), and carefully concludes: "l'ipotesi di una fonte comune sarebbe, genericamente possibile, ma per nulla necessaria" (p. 202). The similarities may be explained by "fashionable" topics of discussion in early fourth-century Athens as, for instance, what makes a citizen useful to the community. For a detailed treatment of the subject, see Lévy, *op. cit.* p. 222ff.; 232ff. and esp. 248ff. On the date of Anon. Iamb. (early fourth century B.C.), see Lévy, *ibid.* p. 91f. It should be stressed that despite the above similarities in subject matter, Aristophanes cannot be said to have shared the views advanced by the anonymous thinker.

[178] *Plut.* 856-9; 863-7; 871.

[179] *Plut.* 904-8.

[180] See above, n. 176.

[181] *Plut.* 924-5. He also states that living a quiet and idle life, without meddling in other people's affairs, is tantamount to living a sheep's life (ll. 922-3); these statements were particularly stressed by Lévy, *op. cit.* p. 236: "il est plus animé par la passion de la politique que par le souci de ses intérêts personnels ... On lui reproche donc moins sa cupidité que sa *polypragmosyne*". It seems to me that this distinction is rather artificial, even if the playwright brought into high relief the sycophant's passion for his "*métier*".

has too often been wrongly interpreted as the political ideal itself, whereas, in fact, it is aimed at the abuse and distortion of this ideal.

This scene in the *Ploutos* reflects certain topics under discussion in Athens at the time of the play's production, with regard to civic ideals and the contribution of the citizens to the community.[182] These topics are closely connected with the salvation theme, which is central in Aristophanes' last plays. It appears that in the playwright's opinion neither the naive *euergesia* of the Honest Man, nor the self-interested, if maniac, "guardianship" of the laws by the sycophant, offers the proper solution to the problems of Athenian society. That is not to say that Aristophanes had the same attitude towards these different patterns of civic behaviour; the Honest Man, as presented by the playwright, deserves human sympathy, though perhaps mingled with pity rather than admiration. Within the context of the dramatic fairy-tale he has to be recompensed for his generosity. On the other hand, the sycophantic disguise of Perikles' political ideal can meet only with profound antipathy. Indeed, the audience is awarded the satisfaction of seeing him driven off the stage in the fury of his political impotence, threatening to bring Wealth to justice for subverting democracy by acting without the consent of the Council and of the Assembly.[183]

Finally, the dominantly social and economic character of Aristophanes' last extant plays implies neither an individualistic or materialistic inclination, nor an apolitical and cosmopolitan mentality on the part of the author. The socio-economic aspect is only a focus of interest which can be explained by the acute problems of the time. But these are, after all, the problems of the Athenian citizens, that is to say, of the Athenian *politeia*, even if treated occasionally, in the *Ploutos*, within a larger scope, Panhellenic or universal.

7. *The Middle Road*

Aristophanes' own socio-economic ideal, implied throughout his last plays, is stated in the most explicit way through the mouth of Poverty: both excessive wealth and abject poverty are destructive to society; the middle way between exaggerated prosperity and degrading pauperism is

---

[182] See above, nn. 176 and 177.

[183] *Plut.* 930-57. The self-interested guardianship of the laws and of democracy by the sycophant may be compared with the attitude of the Hag in *Eccl.* 944-5, though he is obsessed with money and "activism", whereas she is obsessed with sex. All this does not imply that Aristophanes treats laws and democracy with contempt, even if some of their self-interested guardians are depicted as contemptible creatures. On Aristophanes' hostile attitude towards sycophants, see, e.g., *Ach.* 515-22; 559; 679ff.; 818ff.; 839-41; 904ff.; *Eq.* 435ff.; *Vesp.* 1094-6; *Pax*, 190-1; 653; *Av.* 285; 1410ff.; *Eccl.* 452-3; 560-2; *Plut.* 30-1.

the ideal situation for humankind. This is not only an economic creed but a moral attitude towards life. The sympathy towards the *mesotēs* is deeply rooted in Greek consciousness, but Aristophanes was the first who transposed this moral (and political) attitude to economic terms. In order to express his own ideal he has used the ingenious means of ambivalence and has played on the two senses of the word *penia*. On the one hand *penia*, taken as extreme poverty, is "the most destructive beast in the world", "an accursed jade", "the most disgusting creature",[184] and the "blessings" of this abominable monster are summed up by Chremylos in the famous passage quoted above. On the other hand, the allegorical figure of Penia categorically denies the accuracy of the portrait drawn by Chremylos, arguing that it applies to Beggary (Ptocheia). Chremylos' suggestion that Beggary is her sister is also rejected by Poverty. *She* is wholly different: the man who walks in her ways has never suffered and will never suffer the privations enumerated by Chremylos.[185]

Aristophanes seems to have intended to encourage his audience and to hold out the hope that, despite adverse circumstances, despite the grave problems Athens was facing, her economy could still offer to those ready to work hard the possibility of living a modest and decent life, especially if the political leadership was to be taken out of the hands of unworthy leaders (*prostatai ponēroi*)—irresponsible demagogues like Agyrrhios, or incompetent and dishonest politicians, like Neokleides.[186]

It is worth noting that within the argument of Penia, Aristophanes introduces, as if by the way, a political issue: saying that Poverty and Beggary are sisters, she argues, is tantamount to saying that there is no difference between Dionysios the tyrant and Thrasyboulos,[187] the staunch supporter of democracy, who had played a central role in the overthrow of the Thirty Tyrants (i.e., no difference between the tyrant and the deliverer from tyrants). Thrasyboulos had died shortly before the

---

[184] *Plut.* 442-3; 451; 456; 472.

[185] *Plut.* 548-54.

[186] See *Eccl.* 176-7. Neokleides' blindness may be not only a physical defect mocked by Aristophanes out of antipathy for his political behaviour—his arrogance, aggressiveness and dishonesty (*Eccl.* 254; *Plut.* 666; 725)—but also a symbol of the shortsightedness characteristic of many contemporary politicians, whom the playwright thought incapable of coping with the problems of the day. It is significant that Neokleides was the first speaker on the question how to save the state; and the reaction of the people is equally significant when they ask how dare a man who cannot save his own eyesight teach how to save the *polis* (*Eccl.* 395 102). In the *Ploutos*, his blindness is conveniently connected with the problem of Wealth's blindness. He is treated by Asklepios just before Wealth, but whereas the latter is healed, Neokleides' blindness is aggravated, to the satisfaction of the audience (717-26; 747). He is described by the scholiasts to *Eccl.* and *Plut.* (*locc. citt.*) as an orator and an informer. See also Kock, I, fr. 439 (from the *Storks*); cf. J. M. Edmonds, *The Fragments of Attic Comedy* I (Leyden, 1957), p. 697.

[187] *Plut.* 550. See the remarks of Sartori, "Elementi storici" (above n. 1), p. 338ff.

production of the *Ploutos*.[188] A few years before his death he had been for
a time out of favour in Athens: in the *Ekklesiazousai*, it is suggested that
Thrasyboulos, the only man capable of finding a way to *sōtēria*, had been
banished from public life.[189]

Since most of the public figures in Aristophanes' comedies are mocked
in one way or another, the exceptions are particularly noteworthy. In this
case the exception is all the more remarkable since the above-mentioned
passages are not at all funny in themselves and the mention of
Thrasyboulos is in no way necessary from the dramatic point of view,
i.e., as an integral or indispensable component of the plot. This makes it
certain that we are being presented with Aristophanes' own opinion and
not with the viewpoint of a *dramatis persona*.[189a] The playwright can
therefore be said to have nurtured a great admiration for this politician
and to have believed that Athens needed statemanship of his calibre. The
references to Thrasyboulos in Aristophanes' last plays provide an additional example of the poet's ability to combine political topics mentioned
en passant with socio-economic themes.

To return to the latter, the presentation of Chremylos in the *Ploutos* is
highly significant with respect to the ambiguity of Penia. He describes
himself from the very beginning of the play as a poor man, a *penēs*,[190] and
later Poverty confirms this by stating that she had been for many years
the constant companion of himself and his friends.[191] Chremylos' complaints and his bitterness stem, to a considerable extent, from seeing
other citizens grow rich and prosperous in all sorts of evil ways. But
despite his bitterness, despite his presentation of Poverty's "blessings",
which he equates, as we have seen, with the abominable situation of
destitute pauperism, he is not, himself, a pauper, a beggar,[192] nor are his
friends paupers. They own their own property, even slaves—witness

---

[188] He was in charge of a fleet in the eastern Aegean and was murdered when visiting
Aspendos (389 B.C.) by inhabitants of the city (Xen. *Hell.* 4, 8, 30).

[189] *Eccl.* 202-3; cf. Ussher, *Eccl.* p. XXV; 103; 126.

[189a] Since this method was recommended in principle by Ste. Croix, *The Origins of the
Peloponnesian War*, p. 234ff. and 356ff., it is strange that the example of Thrasyboulos
escaped his notice when he spoke of prominent politicians not ridiculed by Aristophanes.
Strange, because this example contradicts his view of the playwright's political outlook
(see esp. *ibid.* p. 361f.).

[190] *Plut.* 29.

[191] *Plut.* 437.

[192] See esp. *Plut.* 247-8; here Chremylos presents himself as a man who joys in thrift as
no other man does and also in spending when it is necessary; cf. Urbain, "Les idées
économiques d'Aristophane" (above, n. 23), p. 186f.: "... un individu, qui, bien qu'
ayant encore de quoi vivre sur les bénéfices d'un effort passé, continue à travailler sans
consommer ce revenu qu'il épargne ... l'homme qui ne vit pas de ses rentes, mais de son
travail".

Karion, Chremylos' slave.[193] However, they have to work hard in their fields in order to earn a living.[194] (It is certainly not accurate to describe them as *bourgeois* or *petits-bourgeois*, as has been done in the literature.[195]) The condition Poverty is defending is not that of degrading pauperism, but of "living a thrifty life, applying oneself to one's work, having nothing superfluous, yet not lacking the necessities either".[196]

Poverty claims that she makes men better than does Wealth, better both in body and mind.[197] She claims responsibility, not only for all moderation and decency,[198] but for all good things in life, including all energy, industry and initiative; without her stimulus, all creative and productive activities would be paralysed: no one would pursue either trade of craft.[199]

There is a passage in the fourth book of the *Republic* in which Plato expresses ideas strikingly similar to those advanced by Aristophanes in the *agōn* of the *Ploutos*. The philosopher states that both wealth and poverty (meaning excessive wealth and abject poverty) have a destructive influence upon artisans as well as upon the products of the arts. A potter who grows rich will no longer be willing to give his mind to the craft; he will become idle and negligent. But if out of extreme poverty he is unable to provide himself with tools and all the requirements of his art, the prod-

---

[193] Perhaps Chremylos had more than one slave. In *Plut.* 26-7, he says that Karion is the most reliable and the best thief (or, the most loyal and the most thievish) τῶν οἰκετῶν, which may be translated either "of the slaves" or "of the household". Later on, in *Plut.* 816ff., Karion mentions his fellow-servants, but this is after his master became rich and may well be part of the dramatic illusion; cf. l. 1105.

[194] *Plut.* 223-4; 253-4; cf. Heitland, *Agricola*, p. 44f.; A. R. Hands, *Charities and Social Aid in Greece and Rome* (London, 1968), p. 62; M. I. Finley, *The Ancient Economy* (London, 1973), p. 41.

[195] See, e.g., Couat, *Aristophane*, p. 197; cf. Ehrenberg, *The People of Aristophanes*, p. 38 and n. 3; 80; 92; 145; 321; 360.

[196] *Plut.* 553-4: "τοῦ δὲ πένητος ζῆν φειδόμενον καὶ τοῖς ἔργοις προσέχοντα, περιγίγνεσθαι δ'αὐτῷ μηδέν, μὴ μέντοι μηδ' ἐπιλείπειν." Cf. Urbain, *op. cit.* p. 187, who calls this economic situation "état de besoin"; Croiset, *Aristophanes*, p. 181, calls it "enforced economy". See also V. Paronzini, "L'ideale politico d'Aristofane", *Dioniso* 11 (1948), p. 36; "A questo mondo borghese si arresta ormai l'ideale aristofanico"; Finley, *loc. cit.* (above, n. 194).

[197] *Plut.* 558-61; 576-8.

[198] *Plut.* 563-4. Her claim is later supported by the significant example of the Honest Man (Dikaios Anēr), whose economic situation had initially been that of the Mean: he inherited an estate perfectly adequate to his needs. His high moral standards as shown by his readiness to help his friends when in need, even at the risk of losing, strengthen Penia's argument that she is an asset to morality.

[199] *Plut.* 510-34. Had Aristophanes really wanted to give Chremylos a fair chance to face Penia with a logical argument, he could have made him argue at this stage of the *agōn*, in perfect consistency with what had already been stated in the play, that Wealth was not intended to give a share to everyone but only to those who deserved it. However, the playwright seems to have preferred to overlook this point, so that he could present Penia's arguments as convincing as possible. See also below, and n. 202.

uct of his work will deteriorate seriously. Thus excessive wealth brings luxury and idleness, whereas extreme poverty brings illiberality and poor craftsmanship. Both of them are said to be detrimental to the stability of the state.[200] It is hard to deny the high probability of Aristophanes' influence on most of these remarks.

There is no solid basis for the argument that Aristophanes, in turn, borrowed here the views expressed in a treatise on Poverty written by some contemporary sophist.[201] After all, the views advanced by Poverty in the *agōn* of the *Ploutos* have, to a considerable extent, been prepared for, by implication, in the *Ekklesiazousai*, in Aristophanes' attack on Praxagora's "communism", which is, among other things, based on parasitic consumption, not on production, just like the ideal society envisaged by Chremylos.

Despite her arguments, Poverty is not able to convince her interlocutors. Moreover, there is no real communication between them, since Chremylos and his friend, Blepsidemos, continue to think of *penia* in their own terms. All Chremylos can ask Poverty after having heard her arguments is whether it is better to be rich or to be hungry. And he adds categorically: "Go away and don't utter one more word. For you won't persuade me even if you do persuade me."[202]

Aristophanes' own opinion about the *agōn* is quite clear: Poverty's arguments are presented as irrefutable; moreover her words contain the main message of the play. As a result, the playwright's decision to banish Poverty from the stage at the end of the *agōn*, and never re-introduce her, has been the cause of embarassment among critics. Some scholars have even accused Aristophanes of self-contradiction and inconsistency.[203]

This approach does not take into account the psychological complexity of the relationship between the playwright and his audience, which, in

---

[200] Plat. *Resp.* 421C-422A.

[201] This view was advanced by G. Meyer, *Laudes Inopiae* (diss. Göttingen, 1915), p. 8f., and later it was adopted by Croiset, *Aristophanes*, p. 181. However, Meyer rightly rejects Gercke's theory that Aristophanes followed Antisthenes' doctrines in the *agōn* of the *Ploutos*: "Antisthenem enim omnis cultus humani adversarium fuisse satis est certum ... Prometheum, quia cum igne etiam initia cultus humani hominibus attulisset, vehementer vituperavit. Apud Aristophanem autem ... Penia, quae homines laborare cogat et ita artificia artesque efficiat, est quasi alter Prometheus" (*ibid.* p. 7).

[202] *Plut.* 595ff.; 599-600.

[203] See, for instance, Croiset, *Aristophanes*, p. 179: "Were the play an argument in favour of slender fortunes, the author ought to have shown us what is lost by becoming rich. On the contrary, he appears to welcome this outcome with satisfaction, and merely seeks to entertain us."; Norwood, *Greek Comedy*, p. 275f.; cf. Greene, "The Comic Technique of Aristophanes" (above, n. 5), p. 124; A. H. Sommerstein in Aristophanes, *Knights* ... (above, n. 91), Intr. to *Wealth*, p. 268; See also T. Long, "Persuasion and the Aristophanic *Agōn*", *TAPA* 103 (1972), p. 285ff., who comes to the conclusion that not only in the *Ploutos* but in Aristophanic comedy in general "the persuasive effect of the *agon* is minimal, its dramatic effect ... almost nonexistent". (p. 297).

this case, seems to have led to Aristophanes' decision to banish Poverty and proceed in the way he did. On the one hand, he had some hard things to say to his audience, and in saying them demonstrated the same courage he had so often displayed in the past. On the other hand, he could not, or did not want to, deprive his audience of a dream, especially after having aroused their expectations. The allegorical figure of Poverty has not only expressed Aristophanes' moral views on society and economics but has also contributed to strengthen the self-confidence and the pride of the poor amongst the audience. However, after having fulfilled her function, Poverty had to vanish because the dream had to go on: the expectations of the public had to be satisfied, the miracle had to occur and the dramatic illusion was not to be broken.

It is hardly possible fully to understand Aristophanes without taking into account his obligation to his *genre* and his relation to his audience. And no guide is better than Aristophanes himself. At the end of the *Ekklesiazousai*, when addressing the audience through the mouth of the Chorus, the playwright asks to be judged by two criteria: "Let the wise choose me for wisdom's sake; let those who enjoy a good laugh choose me for the fun I have given."[204] He should have been entitled to make the same request at the end of the *Ploutos* and add—Let those who enjoy the illusion of a dream choose my play for that illusion, but never forget that there is no shame in poverty; those who work hard for their existence and live an austere life are better than the wealthy.

Aristophanes' socio-economic and moral ideal of the "middle road" was to become one of the cornerstones of Greek political thought during the late-classical period. "Neither surfeit nor want"[205]—this is, in Isokrates' words, the ideal situation for the individual citizen and for the community. Both Plato, in the *Laws*, and Aristotle, in the *Politics*, considered a moderate degree of prosperity, a middle way between excessive wealth and abject poverty—within the framework of an agrarian economy—as the ideal condition for a well-ordered, healthy and viable *politeia*.[206]

---

[204] *Eccl.* 1155-6: "τοῖς σοφοῖς μέν, τῶν σοφῶν μεμνημένοις κρίνειν ἐμέ. τοῖς γελῶσι δ'ἡδέως, διὰ τὸν γέλων κρίνειν ἐμέ.

[205] *Pax*, 90; *Areop.* 3-5: Excessive wealth and power are here said to be accompanied by folly and licence (ἄνοια καὶ ἀκολασία), whereas poverty is said to be attended by sobriety and great moderation (σωφροσύνη καὶ πολλὴ μετριότης). Aristophanes had used exactly the same terms with respect to poverty: see *Plut.* 245 and 563-4.

[206] See Plat. *Leg.* 744D-E; cf. 679B-C; 705B; 706A; 709A and *passim*; Arist. *Pol.* 1265a 29ff.; 1266b 28ff.; 1295b 4ff.; 26ff.; 1326b 30ff.; 1329a 17ff., 1330a 2ff. and *passim*.

BIBLIOGRAPHY

Adam, J., *The Republic of Plato*² I-II (Cambridge, 1963).
Albini, U., *Andocide, De pace* (Firenze, 1964).
——, "La struttura del *Pluto* di Aristofane", *PP* 20 (1965), 427ff.
Barker, E., *Greek Political Theory. Plato and his Predecessors*³ (London, 1964).
Barrett, D. and Sommerstein, A. H., *The Knights, Peace, the Birds, the Assemblywomen, Wealth* (Harmondsworth, Penguin, 1978).
Beloch, K. J., *Griechische Geschichte*² III, i (Berlin-Leipzig, 1922).
Busolt, G. (and Swoboda, H.), *Griechische Staatskunde*³ I (München, 1920).
Cantarella, R., "L'ultimo Aristofane", *Dioniso* 40 (1966), 35ff.
Cassio, A. C., Review of: R. G. Ussher, *Aristophanes, Ecclesiazusae* (*q.v.*), *RFIC* 103 (1975), 73ff.
Cataudella, Q., "Due note ad Aristofane", *Athen.* 13 (1935), 195ff.
Chiapelli, A., "Le *Ecclesiazusae* di Aristofane e la *Repubblica* di Platone", *Riv. Fil.* 11 (1883), 161ff.
Cloché, P., "La démocratie athénienne et les possédants aux vᵉ et ivᵉ siècles avant J.-C.", *RH* 192 (1941), 1ff.
Couat, A., *Aristophane et l'ancienne comédie attique* (Paris, 1902).
Coulon, V., "Notes sur l'*Assemblée des femmes* d'Aristophane", *REG* 36 (1923), 367ff.
—— and Van Daele, H., *Aristophane* V. *L'Assemblée des femmes, Ploutos*⁴ (Paris, Budé, 1963).
Croiset, M., *Aristophanes and the Political Parties at Athens*, translated by J. Loeb (London, 1909).
David, E., "The Spartan *Syssitia* and Plato's Laws", *AJP* 99 (1978), 486ff.
——, *Sparta between Empire and Revolution (404-243 B.C.). Internal Problems and their Impact on Contemporary Greek Consciousness* (New York, Arno, 1981).
Davies, J. K., *Athenian Propertied Families, 600-300 B.C.* (Oxford, 1971).
Demiańczuk, J., *Supplementum Comicum* (Cracow, 1912).
Dickinson, P., *Aristophanes: The Plays* II (Oxford, 1970).
Diels, H. and Kranz, W., *Die Fragmente der Vorsokratiker*⁶ II (Berlin, 1952).
Diès, A., *Platon, La République* (Paris, Budé, 1947).
Dover, K. J., *Aristophanic Comedy* (Berkeley and Los Angeles, 1972).
Dübner, F., *Scholia Graeca in Aristophanem* (Paris, 1842).
Edmonds, J. H., *The Fragments of Attic Comedy* I (Leyden, 1957).
Ehrenberg, V., "Pericles and his Colleagues", *AJP* 66 (1945), 113ff.
——, "Polypragmosyne: A Study in Greek Politics", *JHS* 67 (1947), 46ff.
——, *The People of Aristophanes. A Sociology of Old Attic Comedy*² (Oxford, 1951).
Field, G. C., *Plato and his Contemporaries*³ (London, 1967).
Finley, M. I., *The Ancient Economy* (London, 1973).
——, "Utopianism, Ancient and Modern", in *The Use and Abuse of History* (London, 1975).
Forrest, W. G., "Aristophanes and the Athenian Empire", in Levick, B., ed., *The Ancient Historian and His Materials. Essays in Honour of C. E. Stevens on his Seventieth Birthday* (Farnborough, 1975).
Fraenkel, E., "Dramaturgical Problems in the *Ecclesiazusae*", in *Greek Poetry and Life: Essays Presented to G. Murray on his Seventieth Birthday* (Oxford, 1936), 257ff.
Francotte, H., *Les finances des cités grecques* (Paris, 1909).
Frey, V., "Zur Komödie des Aristophanes", *MH* 5 (1948), 168ff.
Fuks, A., "Isokrates and the Social-Economic Situation in Greece", *Anc. Soc.* 3 (1972), 17ff.
——, "Patterns and Types of Social-Economic Revolution in Greece from the Fourth to the Second Century B.C.", *Anc. Soc.* 5 (1974), 51ff.

——, "The Conditions of 'Riches' and 'Poverty' in Plato's *Republic*", *RSA* 6/7 (1976/7), 63ff.

——, "Plato and the Social Question: The Problem of Poverty and Riches in the *Republic*", *Anc. Soc.* 8 (1977), 49ff.

——, "Plato and the Social Question: The Problem of Poverty and Riches in the *Laws*", *Anc. Soc.* 10 (1979), 33ff.

——, "The Sharing of Property by the Rich with the Poor in Greek Theory and Practice", *SCI* 5 (1979/80), 46ff.

Gelzer, Th., *RE* Suppl. XII (1970), s.v. "Aristophanes", coll. 1391ff.

Gigante, M., "Echi di vita politica nelle *Ecclesiazusae* di Aristofane", *Dioniso* 11 (1948), 147ff.

Glotz, G., *Le travail dans la Grèce ancienne* (Paris, 1920).

Gomme, A. W., "Aristophanes and Politics", *CR* 52 (1938), 97ff., repr. in *id. More Essays in Greek History and Literature* (Oxford, 1962).

Green, W. C., *The Plutus of Aristophanes* (Cambridge, 1892).

Greene, D., "The Comic Technique of Aristophanes", *Hermathena* 50 (1937), 87ff.

Hamilton, C. D., *Sparta's Bitter Victories. Politics and Diplomacy in the Corinthian War* (Ithaca, N.Y., Cornell Univ. Press, 1979).

Hands, A. R., *Charities and Social Aid in Greece and Rome* (London, 1968).

Heitland, W. E., *Agricola. A Study of Agriculture and Rustic Life in the Graeco-Roman World from the Point of View of Labour* (Cambridge, 1921).

Hess, W. H., *Studies in the Ecclesiazusae of Aristophanes* (diss. Princeton, 1963).

Holzinger, K., *Kritisch-exegetischer Kommentar zu Aristophanes' Plutos* (Wien-Leipzig, 1940).

Hugill, W. M., *Panhellenism in Aristophanes* (diss. Chicago, 1936).

Jacoby, F., *Fragmente der griechischen Historiker* (Berlin-Leyden, 1923-).

Kock, Th., *Comicorum Atticorum Fragmenta* I (Leipzig, 1880).

Koster, W. J. W., *Naar aanleiding van het communisme bij Aristophanes en Plato* (Groningen, (1955).

Lana, I., "Le teorie equalitarie di Falea di Calcedone", *Rivista critica di storia della filosofia* (1950), 265ff.

Lévy, E., *Athènes devant la défaite de 404. Histoire d'une crise idéologique*, Bibl. des Écoles Françaises d'Athènes et de Rome, 225 (Paris, 1976).

——, "Les femmes chez Aristophane", *Ktema* 1 (1976), 99ff.

Long, T., "Persuasion and the Aristophanic Agon", *TAPA* 103 (1972), 285ff.

Luccioni, J., *La pensée politique de Platon* (Paris, 1958).

MacDowell, D. M., Review of: R. G. Ussher, *Aristophanes, Ecclesiazusae* (*q.v.*), *JHS* 94 (1974), 184f.

Mactoux, M.-M., *Douleia. Esclavage et pratiques discursives dans l'Athènes classique* (Paris, 1980).

Mahaffy, J. P., *Social Life in Greece from Homer to Menander* (London, 1898).

McLeish, K., *Clouds, Women in Power, Knights* (Cambridge, 1979).

Meyer, W., *Laudes Inopiae* (diss. Göttingen, 1915).

Mossé, C., *La fin de la démocratie athénienne* (Paris, 1962).

Murray, G., *Aristophanes: A Study* (Oxford, 1933).

Nauck, A., *Tragicorum Graecorum Fragmenta*² (Leipzig, 1889: repr. Hildesheim, 1964).

Newman, W. L., *The Politics of Aristotle* I-IV (Oxford, 1887-1902).

Nicosia, G., *Economia e Politica di Atene attraverso Aristofane* (Milano, 1935).

Norwood, G., *Greek Comedy* (London, 1931).

Ollier, F., *Le mirage spartiate I: Étude sur l'idéalisation de Sparte dans l'antiquité grecque de l'origine jusqu'aux cyniques* (Paris, 1933).

Page, D. L., *Greek Literary Papyri* I (London, Loeb, 1942).

—— *Epigrammata Graeca* (Oxford, 1975).

Parker, D., *The Congresswomen* (Ann Arbor, 1967).

Paronzini, V., "L'ideale politico d'Aristofane", *Dioniso* 11 (1948), 26ff.

Perlman, S., "The Causes and Outbreak of the Corinthian War", *CQ* 4 (1964), 64ff.

Pöhlmann, R. Von, *Geschichte der sozialen Frage und des Sozialismus in der antiken Welt* II (München, 1925).

Pohlenz, M., *Aus Platos Werdezeit* (Berlin, 1913).
Quinn, M. T., *The Plutus of Aristophanes* (London, 1901).
Radin, M., "Freedom of Speech in Ancient Athens", *AJP* 48 (1927), 219ff.
Radt, S. L., "Aristophanes' *Plutus*", *Lampas* 11 (1978), 2ff.
Rogers, B. B., *The Ecclesiazusae of Aristophanes* (London, 1902).
—— *The Plutus of Aristophanes* (London, 1907).
—— *Aristophanes* III (London, Loeb, 1924).
Roos, E., "De exodi Ecclesiazusarum fabulae ratione et consilio", *Eranos* 49 (1951), 5ff.
Russo, C. F., *Aristofane autore di teatro* (Firenze, 1962).
Ryder, T. T. B., *Koine Eirene. General Peace and Local Independence in Ancient Greece* (Oxford, 1965).
Ste. Croix G. E. M. de, *The Origins of the Peloponnesian War* (London, 1972).
Sartori, F., "Elementi storici del tardo teatro aristofanico e documentazione contemporanea", in Akten des VI. internationalen Kongresses für griechische und lateinische Epigraphik, *Vestigia* 17 (München, 1973), 328ff.
Schreiber, F., Review of: R. G. Ussher, *Aristophanes, Ecclesiazusae* (*q.v.*), *AJP* 96 (1975), 308f.
Sommerstein, A. H. - see under Barrett, D.
Strauss, L., *Socrates and Aristophanes* (New York, 1966).
Taillardat, J., *Les images d'Aristophane*² (Paris, 1965).
Taylor, A. E., *Plato. The Man and his Work* (London, 1926).
Thomsen, R., *Eisphora. A Study of Direct Taxation in Ancient Athens* (Copenhagen, 1964).
Tigerstedt, E. N., *The Legend of Sparta in Classical Antiquity* I (Stockholm, 1965).
Urbain, Y., "Les idées économiques d'Aristophane", *AC* 8 (1939), 183ff.
Ussher, R. G., "The Staging of the Ecclesiazusae", *Hermes* 97 (1969), 22ff.
—— *Aristophanes, Ecclesiazusae* (Oxford, 1973).
—— *Aristophanes*, in Greece and Rome, New Surveys in the Classics, No. 13 (Oxford, 1979).
Van Daele, H. - see under Coulon, V.
Van Leeuwen, J., *Aristophanis Ecclesiazusae* (Leyden, 1905).
—— *Prolegomena ad Aristophanem* (Leyden, 1908).
Vidal-Naquet, P., "Esclavage et gynécocratie dans la tradition, le mythe, l'utopie", *Recherches sur les structures sociales dans l'antiquité classique* (Paris, 1970).
Webster, T. B. L., *Studies in Later Greek Comedy*² (Manchester, 1970).
Whitman, C. H., *Aristophanes and the Comic Hero* (Cambridge, Mass., 1964).
Wilamowitz-Moellendorff, U. von, *Aristophanes Lysistrate, Beilage: Ekklesiazusen* (Berlin, 1927).
Willems, A., *Aristophane* III (Paris-Bruxelles, 1919).
Wilson, N. G., Review of: R. G. Ussher, *Aristophanes, Ecclesiazusae* (*q.v.*), *CR* 26 (1976), 12ff.
Wit-Tak, Th. M. de, Review of: R. G. Ussher, *Aristophanes, Ecclesiazusae* (*q.v.*) *Mnemosyne* 30 (1977), 83f.
Zuccante, G., "Aristofane e Platone", *RIL* 62 (1929), 380ff.

Printed in the United States
By Bookmasters